CONTAGIOUS COMMUNITY

LIVING BEYOND YOURSELF

Connect with God. Connect with Others.
Connect with Life.

Contagious Community: Living Beyond Yourself
Youth Edition Leader Book

Nashville, Tennessee

ISBN: 9781574944310
Item Number: 005125108

Dewey Decimal Classification: 307
Subject Headings:
COMMUNITY LIFE \ CHURCH FELLOWSHIP

Printed in the United States of America

Student Ministry Publishing
LifeWay Church Resources
One LifeWay Plaza
Nashville, TN 37234-0174

We believe that the Bible has God for its author, salvation for its end; and truth, without any mixture of error, for its matter and that all Scripture is totally true and trustworthy. The 2000 statement of *The Baptist Faith and Message* is our doctrinal guideline.

CONTENTS

Life Connections® YOUTH Experience

Combine teaching that engages a large-group with dynamic small-group experiences and discussions and the result is students grappling with reality and real life change. Throughout 13 sessions, small groups will find power in just being together in community. Help them connect with God . . . connect with each other . . . connect with life! Each session consists of a four-part agenda. In addition, "Get Ready" and "Now What?" segments enable students to dig a little deeper and give God more opportunity to impact their lives.

Get Ready

To get the most from this experience, students should spend time with God each day leading up to the session. They simply wrap their brains around the short Bible passages, listen to God, and jot down thoughts and insights.

So What?

The Master Teacher will lead the entire group in understanding what God has to say on the topic. Content has biblical depth, yet is engaging. Students can follow along, jot notes, and respond to questions in their student books.

LifePoint

Welcome and communicate the "LifePoint" or big idea for the session, and then divide students into small groups. NOTE: If feasible, keep the same groups together each week to enhance the depth of group dynamic and potential for life change.

Do What?

All study should direct us toward action and life change. The goal in small groups is to be real with each other in order to connect with God, with others, and with life. Students will find power to integrate truth into life with the support and prayers of other students.

Say What?

Small-group facilitators lead students in interactive experiences and discussions. "Random Question of the Week" will open students up and encourage them to join activities or discussions that lead into the session topic.

Now What?

To see real power in life, encourage students not to just leave the session and go on as normal. The "Now What?" assignments help them continue their journeys and give them opportunity to go deeper with God.

Life Connections® Youth At a Glance

Get Ready

Daily time with God
& your journal

LifePoint

Large Group:
welcome & theme

Say What?

Small Group:
fun & interaction

So What?

Large Group:
teaching & discovery
(Master Teacher)

Do What?

Small Group:
getting real
& connecting

Now What?

Continue your journey . . .

LEADERS AND FACILITATORS

Every Life Connections group must fill three important roles. Each responsibility is vital to the success of the class.

Teacher—The teacher is the key leader of any Life Connections group.
It is the responsibility of the teacher to:

1. enlist facilitators and apprentices.
2. make facilitators and apprentices aware of their roles and be certain these responsibilities are carried out.
3. meet periodically with facilitators to train, encourage, and inspire them.
4. cast vision for and keep the group focused on the goals of the group.
5. guide group members to understand and commit to the group covenant.
6. be sure the group utilizes, fills, and evangelizes through use of the empty chair concept.
7. act as the Master Teacher for the group.
8. keep the group on task throughout each session.

Facilitator—Each subgroup will have a facilitator. It is the responsibility of the facilitators to:

1. lead each individual in their subgroup to participate in "Say What?" activities.
2. guide those in their subgroup to commit to apply the lessons learned in the "Do What?" section of the weekly session.
3. lead their subgroup to support one another with sensitivity and wisdom during the "Do What?" closing and involve their subgroup in ministry and evangelism.
4. encourage students to go deeper by completing the "Get Ready" and "Now What?" times on their own between sessions.
5. minister to the needs of their subgroup members and lead them to minister to the needs of one another both during and between meetings.

Apprentice—Every subgroup must have an apprentice. When the group consistently has eight or more in attendance, the group should divide into two groups. The apprentice will become the facilitator of the new group and choose an apprentice who will someday be the facilitator of a group. It is the role of the apprentice to:

1. learn from the facilitator of the group.
2. make welcome all new subgroup members.
3. be certain student books, pens or pencils, and other supplies are available for all students.
4. turn in prayer requests.
5. encourage participation by actively participating.
6. lead the group when the facilitator is unavailable.

CORE VALUES

Community:
God is relational, so He created us to live in relationship with Him and each other. Authentic community involves sharing life together and connecting on many levels with the people in our group.

Group Process:
Developing authentic community requires a step-by-step process. It's a journey of sharing our stories with each other and learning together.

Interactive Bible Study:
God provided the Bible as an instruction manual of life. We need to deepen our understanding of God's Word. People learn and remember more as they wrestle with truth and learn from others. The process of Bible discovery and group interaction will enhance our growth.

Experiential Growth:
The goal of studying the Bible together is not merely a quest for knowledge; this should result in real life change. Beyond solely reading, studying, and dissecting the Bible, being a disciple of Christ involves reunifying knowledge with experience. We do this by bringing our questions to God, opening a dialogue with our hearts (instead of killing our desires), and utilizing other ways to listen to God speak to us (group interaction, nature, art, movies, circumstances, and so forth). Experiential growth is always grounded in the Bible as God's primary means of revelation and our ultimate source of truth.

The Power of God:
Our processes and strategies will be ineffective unless we invite and embrace God's presence and power. In order to experience community and growth, Jesus must be the centerpiece of our group experiences and the Holy Spirit must be at work.

Redemptive Community:
Healing best happens within the context of community and in relationship. A key aspect of our spiritual development is seeing ourselves through the eyes of others, sharing our stories, and ultimately being set free from the secrets and the lies we embrace that enslave our souls.

Mission:
God has invited us into a larger story with a great mission. It is a mission that involves setting captives free and healing the broken hearted (Isaiah 61:1-2). However, we can only join in this mission to the degree that we've let Jesus bind up our wounds and set us free. As a group experiences true redemptive community, other people will be attracted to that group, and through that group to Jesus. We should be alert to inviting others while we maintain (and continue to fill) an "empty chair" in our meetings to remind us of others who need to encounter God and authentic Christian community.

GROUP COVENANT

It is important that your group covenant together, agreeing to live out important group values. Once these values are agreed upon, your group will be on its way to experiencing true Christian community. It's very important that your group discuss these values—preferably as you begin this study. The first session would be most appropriate. (Check the rules to which each member of your group agrees.)

☐ Priority: While you are in this course of study, you give the group meetings priority.

☐ Participation: Everyone is encouraged to participate and no one dominates.

☐ Respect: Everyone is given the right to his or her own opinion, and all questions are encouraged and respected.

☐ Confidentiality: Anything that is said in the meeting is never repeated outside the meeting without permission. Note: Church staff may be required by law to report illegal activities.

☐ Life Change: We will regularly assess our own progress in applying "LifePoints" and encourage one another in our pursuit of becoming more like Christ.

☐ Care and Support: Permission is given to call upon each other at any time, especially in times of crisis. The group will provide care for every member.

☐ Accountability: We agree to let the members of the group hold us accountable to the commitments we make in whatever loving ways we decide upon. Unsolicited advice giving is not permitted.

☐ Empty Chair: The group is open to welcoming new people at every meeting.

☐ Mission: We agree as a group to reach out and invite others to join us.

☐ Ministry: We will encourage one another to volunteer and serve in a ministry and to support missions by giving financially and/or personally serving.

Session 1

THE CONTAGIOUS CHRISTIAN COMMUNITY

Connections Prep

MAIN "LIFEPOINT": The authentic Christian community is contagious.

To reinforce the "LifePoint," leaders and small-group facilitators should understand the following more detailed CheckPoints and "Do" Points.

BIBLE STUDY CHECKPOINTS:

- Understand what an authentic Christian community is according to Acts 2.
- Help people understand how the authentic Christian community can help fill their lives with meaning and acceptance rather than loneliness.
- Evaluate ways to begin to create an atmosphere of authentic Christian community that teenagers want to be a part of.

LIFE CHANGE "DO" POINTS:

- Find an authentic Christian community.
- Commit to being contagious about your faith.
- Do your best to make others comfortable in your Christian community.

PREPARATION:

- ☐ Review the leader book for this session and prepare your teaching in advance.
- ☐ Determine how you will divide students into small discussion groups.
- ☐ Recruit mature students or adults as small-group facilitators. Be sure these facilitators plan to attend your meeting.

REQUIRED SUPPLIES:

- ☐ *Contagious Community: Living Beyond Yourself* leader book for each group facilitator
- ☐ *Contagious Community: Living Beyond Yourself* student book for each student
- ☐ Pen or pencil for each student

"Get Ready" is primarily for students, but leaders and facilitators will benefit from these devotionals as well.

Get Ready

Read one of these short Bible passages each day, and spend a few minutes of focused time with God. Be sure to jot down any insights you receive.

MONDAY

Read Acts 2:42.

If someone were to spend a day with you, to what would they say that you are devoted? Why? With whom do you spend your days? What do you look forward to doing each day?

TUESDAY

Read Acts 2:43.

What is the last thing you saw that really blew your mind? What is something that caused you to be "filled with awe"?

WEDNESDAY

Read Acts 2:44-45.

What is the last item that you shared with someone else? When you share something, do you expect it back? Why or why not? What is the last item that you gave away? What is the most important thing you possess? Would you willingly give it to someone in need?

THURSDAY

Read Acts 2:46.

When was the last time you ate with someone other than at the cafeteria? How did that meal impact you? Is sharing a meal with someone something that helps you build community with others? Why or why not?

FRIDAY

Read Acts 2:47.

When was the last time you gave God thanks? What was the last thing you thanked God for? What is something special that you can do today to show God how thankful you are for what He has blessed you with?

SATURDAY

Read Acts 4:32.
Who are the people with whom you feel "at one?" What makes you feel this way about these people?

SUNDAY

Read Acts 4:33-35.
Who are some people you know who are in need? What are you doing to help them? Is there anything you can do to help them during this time of need?

LARGE-GROUP OPENING:
Get everyone's attention. Make announcements. Open your session with a prayer. Read the "LifePoint" to students.

LifePoint

The authentic Christian community is contagious.

SMALL-GROUP TIME:
Instruct students to divide into groups of four to eight, preferably in a circle configuration.

Call on the mature student or adult leaders you recruited to facilitate each small group through this "Say What?" segment.

Say What? (15 minutes)

Random Question of the Week:
If you were going on a trip, what is one item you would make sure you didn't forget?

Group Experience: "Community" Questions
Share the following "community" questions with the students in your small group and allow each student to answer. Encourage students to share their answers to the questions. The purpose of this experience is to allow students to share their thoughts with the group and also begin thinking about the groups with whom they spend their time.

1. Think about the people with whom you hang out. How would you describe them? Are they:
   - ☐ Jocks
   - ☐ Popular people . . . the "in" group
   - ☐ Nerds and geeks
   - ☐ Just a group of people who like to hang around together
   - ☐ A group of guys looking for girls or vice versa
   - ☐ A group of friends who like to talk about everything
   - ☐ A group who likes to look for adventure
   - ☐ People who encourage me to walk daily with Christ
   - ☐ I hate other people . . . I don't want friends
   - ☐ Other ____________________

2. When you hang out with your friends, where do you hang out? Why do you choose to hang out there?

3. Is there anyone in your group of friends whom you would recognize as the group's "leader"? Why would you recognize that person as the leader of your group? What kind of leader is that person?

LARGE-GROUP TIME: **Direct students to turn to face the front for this teaching time. Be sure you can make eye contact with each student in the room. Encourage them to follow along and take notes in their student books.**

Share the "So What?" information with students. You may modify it to meet your needs. Be sure to highlight the underlined information, which gives answers to the student book questions and fill-in-the-blanks (shown in the margins).

So What? (30 minutes)

Teaching Outline

I. Becoming Contagious
- A. What is an authentic community?
- B. How does something become contagious?
- C. The affect of our attitude on our contagious community

II. Learning from the Bible
Acts 2:42-47

III. The Early Church
- A. A common relationship with Christ
- B. An attitude that motivates
- C. A place of joy and celebration

IV. Shared Resources

A. Sold possessions

B. Spend time

V. Shared Life Experiences

A. Share meals

B. Be yourself

VI. Shared Beliefs

A. Devoted to teaching, prayer, and praising God

B. Devoted to sharing the message of Christ

1

Becoming Contagious

❶ What is the definition of authentic?

After the "Group Experience," ask: **What makes something *authentic* to you?** Today a buzzword in the Christian community is the word *authentic.* ❶ *Authentic* is defined as *not false or copied; genuine; real.* When we hear the word *authentic* today, especially in church, we usually think about something that is genuine or real as the definition above suggests.

When you hear the word *contagious* what do you think of? Do you think of a disease? Do you think of something like leprosy, which the Bible talks about many times? Do you think of a place where lepers are put so they won't infect the rest of the town, something like a leper colony? Do you think of a smile? A smile can be contagious. Do you think of Christianity? What?? How can Christianity be contagious?

❷ How does something become contagious?

Think about a "viral video" that you might have seen recently. You know the kind, the one where the cat falls off the television while it is sleeping or the one where the guy hides in a trash can and scares kids as they walk by. These kinds of videos come to you weekly through your e-mail in-box. You might think that this particular video is one of the funniest videos ever. You wouldn't choose to delete that video then would you? No! You would forward the e-mail to at least one of your friends. If it was a really good video, then you might just forward it to your entire address book! That's how we might view something today as contagious. ❷ In order for something to be contagious, it must come in contact with people. That's why the doctor tells you to stay at home when you're sick so you won't infect others with your contagious sickness. That's why Jesus tells us to go out into the world, so we can be contagious with His message to others. What good is it for us to be contagious with our Christian faith if we sit in our rooms all day?

When we think about the Christian community, we might think about something that is limited to the church or to people who go to church. How many people outside the church could actually enjoy what goes on inside the church? ❸ If we don't have an attitude that motivates us to tell others about how important our relationship is with Christ and other Christians, others will not want anything to do with Christianity. How important is our Christian community?

❸ How can your attitude be a part of Christianity becoming contagious to others?

Scripture tells us about something that spread extremely fast, and it wasn't even a video! The early church was a faith community that turned out to be highly authentic and contagious. ❹ In Acts 2:41, 3000 people "caught" it at once. This contagious community was far from the leper colony where lepers were forced to be. This contagious community was a place of joy and celebration, because what people caught was life-giving rather than life-destroying. The process of catching on was the opposite of disease; those who had been sick were now healed.

❹ According to Acts 2:41, how many people "caught" the gospel message at once?

Before the session, enlist a youth to read Acts 2:42-47.

Learning from the Bible

42 And they devoted themselves to the apostles' teaching, to fellowship, to the breaking of bread, and to prayers.

43 Then fear came over everyone, and many wonders and signs were being performed through the apostles. 44 Now all the believers were together and had everything in common. 45 So they sold their possessions and property and distributed the proceeds to all, as anyone had a need. 46 And every day they devoted themselves to meeting together in the temple complex, and broke bread from house to house. They ate their food with gladness and simplicity of heart, 47 praising God and having favor with all the people. And every day the Lord added to them those who were being saved.

The Early Church

The contagious community that had its beginning in Acts continues to spread throughout the world. Think about it, this contagious community grew by people telling others face to face—no Internet, no e-mail, and no phone calls. ❺ This community grew because people were contagious about the way their lives were changed due to a common relationship with Christ. They didn't choose to sit around with each other in a "holy huddle" and rejoice that they weren't outside. Instead the people were so changed by their relationship with Christ and with each other that they went out and took the message to those outside their Christian community.

❺ How did people in early church times hear about the early contagious Christian community?

Scripture gives us different directions on what we should do for one another, and these will be the basis of our future sessions: accept one another, love one another, show patience with one another, bear one another's burdens, work with one another, forgive one another, be generous with one another, teach one another, live at peace with one another, pray for one another, be thankful for one another, and rejoice with one another. When we do these things as a community of faith, we do our part to create an authentic Christian community that others desire to be a part of. An authentic Christian community doesn't try to hide behind the walls of the church building; instead, to a certain extent, the community tears down the walls and chooses to meet the needs of others. An authentic Christian community won't be keeping people out; rather it won't be able to keep them away.

Today many people experience loneliness. In part, many people experience this loneliness because they don't have a close group of people to interact with. In a recent movie, one of the characters notes that people seldom touch anyone anymore. The character goes on to add, "I think we miss that touch so much that we crash into each other just so we can feel something." The early church did not experience this loneliness because they touched each other. (Not in a sexual way, but in a respectable way that met physical touch needs.) They also responded to the needs they saw in each other.

❻ What three things did the early church share that led to the creation of a contagious community?

The early church built a loving community that met each others needs, and this community became contagious to those outside the community. ❻ As we look at the passage of Scripture, we see the early church shared three things that created a contagious community—beliefs, life experiences, and resources. We will look at these in reverse order.

❼ How was the way the early church gave to the needy different from how most churches give to the needy today?

Shared Resources

The early church members put all of their resources together and shared them. ❼ Verse 45 states, "So they sold their possessions and property and distributed the proceeds to all, as anyone had a need." Many churches have a fund to help people who are in need, but the early church decided that this wasn't enough. They took it a step further and sold their possessions in order to get others the money they needed. This means they didn't give their leftover clothes or what went out of season last year; they gave up their own stuff in order to help others who didn't have anything. They didn't give from what was left over at the end of the month or go to their parents and ask for money for their friends; they sold their own stuff. They didn't get rid of their junk. Their society was much different than ours. They didn't live in a society that put value on accumulating things, rather they lived in a society that put value on people. This commitment to helping each other was noticed by those outside the Christian community and they were contagious. In fact, these acts of help for others helped some come to faith in Christ. Think about the next time you expect to get a present, whether on your birthday or Christmas. Would you be willing to let that gift go so it could either be sold or given to someone else? Your willingness helps determine how attached you are to your stuff.

8 In response to other's hurts, what should we share with them besides our money?

Not every church has its members sell all their possessions in order to have a contagious sense of community. What churches today need to show is a sacrificial commitment to respond to the needs of the people around them. This sacrifice is more than tossing a few coins into the offering plate as it passes, so someone else can help those who are hurting. 8 In response to the hurting needs of others we need to share our time with those in need. Time is often viewed as more precious than money by some because it is easier to give a few leftover dollars to a project than it is to actually roll up our sleeves and get dirty. We can listen to those who need someone to talk to. We can offer to go with our friends to talk to an adult about the things that hurt them. We can even give up our time on a Saturday afternoon to go and sit with those who don't have a family or the elderly in a retirement home. We have the opportunity and the resources to share with others and these shared resources help our Christian community become contagious to others.

Shared Life Experiences

9 What is it about being in a person's home that helps us get to know that person better than we might in a church building or social setting?

The early church also shared their life experiences with each other. Verse 46 states that they "broke bread from house to house" and "ate their food with gladness and simplicity of heart." We might not think that is a big deal. We eat with people every day, especially when we sit in a school cafeteria. This verse means more than simply sharing a meal, it means that they had time in each other's homes. Think about the last time you went to someone's house. What did you notice? Did you see the pictures on the wall? Did you see their family? Did you see where they live? 9 When we enter into the home of someone else, we begin to realize what their life is like. We notice the things that they consider to be important. We recognize if family is important to them. We see the environment that has shaped them into who they are, and we can learn how to pray for them.

10 What are three components to a contagious community?

As Christians, it is important for us to be involved in others' lives rather than hiding away from the outside world in our rooms. Many of us today are much more comfortable hiding away than being with others. Others have hurt us all and that's no secret. Many people choose to become reclusive because they do not want to experience that again. 10 A contagious community of Christians should be a place where we can let our guard down. It must be a place where we can be ourselves, a place where we can be encouraged to tell our own stories and a place where others view us as God created us. When we learn to do that, we will begin to have living and breathing friends, not just those on the television screen.

Shared Beliefs

The people of the early church described in Acts 2 shared together in learning about Jesus Christ. Verse 42 states, "they devoted themselves to the apostles' teaching." This is more than going to church, going to a worship service, or listening to a sermon. The key word is "devoted." This means that they weren't merely on the verge of getting involved in their relationship with Christ, rather, they were consumed by it. ⓫ At the heart of their contagious Christian community was the fact that they devoted themselves to three things: the apostles' teaching, prayer, and praising God together. They were about growing in their relationship with Christ. They weren't satisfied just knowing the answers in their heads, they wanted everything about their lives to be changed because of their relationship with Christ.

⓫ To what three things did the church community in Acts devote themselves?

⓬ How did the early community of Christians become contagious?

⓬ This community of Christians became contagious because they were intentional about telling people the life-changing message of Christ. They taught those who were condemned by the self-righteousness of the religious elite that Jesus loves them just as they are, and they offered forgiveness to them. They taught slaves and women, who were treated as worthless commodities in the society, that Jesus saw them as being so valuable that He would die for them. They made it a point not to discriminate against anyone because they saw everyone as worthy of hearing the good news that had been offered to them. Their community became contagious because people wanted to know about the hope that they had. When you find something out that is interesting, you share it with others. When you find out something that is life changing, do you share it as well?

The early Christian community was genuine with their faith and because they were genuine, their community became contagious. Our passage concludes with the words, "And every day the Lord added to them those who were being saved" (v. 47). They couldn't keep quiet about the great things that God was doing in their midst. They had to tell others. They would not keep quiet. They weren't worried about offending anyone with the message. Their community was more concerned with telling others about what was happening in their lives than they were concerned about who might get mad at them. When we share the same beliefs with a community of Christians we will become more contagious as God works in our lives.

SMALL-GROUP TIME: After presenting the teaching material, ask students to divide back into groups and discuss the "Do What?" questions. Small-group facilitators should lead the discussions and set the model for being open and honest in responding to questions.

Do What? (15 minutes)

Making It Personal

1. What does the word "devoted" mean to you? How does someone show their devotion genuinely?

2. How devoted would you say you are to the things of Christ?

3. What area of your life causes you to struggle the most in regards to Christian community?
   - ☐ I don't feel like I'm important to the group.
   - ☐ I don't feel like anyone else experiences the same struggles that I do.
   - ☐ I wish that I was better at making others feel like they were a part of the group.
   - ☐ I like everyone . . . in fact I'm more concerned about them than God.
   - ☐ Other ______________________________

4. Complete this sentence: If I could change one thing about the Christian community I am a part of, I would . . .

Small-group facilitators should reinforce the "LifePoint" for this session, making sure that students' questions are invited and addressed honestly.

LifePoint Review

The authentic Christian community is contagious.

"Do" Points

These "Do" Points will help you begin to experience this week's "LifePoint." Be open and honest as you discuss the action points within your small group.

1. Find an authentic Christian community. If you don't have a place where you feel comfortable being you, you will never experience all that God intended for you to experience in a Christian community. If you don't find an authentic Christian community, you will not have the opportunity to share your excitement, hopes, and fears with others in a safe environment.

2. Commit to being contagious about your faith. Much like on Christmas day, we tend to tell others about things in our lives that mean something to us. The chance is great that you chose to either call, text, or e-mail someone on Christmas to let them know what great presents you received. Commit to being contagious with your faith in Christ as well.

3. Do your best to make others comfortable in your Christian community. What do you do when you go somewhere and you feel like you don't belong? You probably look for an easy escape or plan an early departure. We all do it. Look around your church in the future. Look for people who are having a hard time finding a place to connect with others. Ask God if you can be of help getting these people plugged into your Christian community.

Encourage students to list prayer needs for others in their books so they can pray for one another during the week.

Assign a student coordinator in each small group to gather the group's requests and e-mail them to the group members.

Prayer Connection:

This is the time to encourage, support, and pray for each other in our journeys to trust God and seek out real and personal encounters with Him.

Share prayer needs and requests with the group, especially those related to hearing from and responding to God. Your group facilitator will close your time in prayer.

Prayer Needs:

Encourage students to dig a little deeper by completing a "Now What?" assignment before the next time you meet.

Remind students about the "Get Ready" short daily Bible readings and related questions at the beginning of session 2.

Now What?

Remind them again this week that they are loved!

Deepen your understanding of who God is and His desire for us to have an authentic Christian community, and continue the journey you've begun today by choosing one of the following assignments to complete this week:

Option #1:

If you enjoy writing, take the time this week to keep a journal about the times when you interact with others. Note the people with whom you interact and with whom you feel most comfortable. Note the places that you go with your friends and note the places where you feel most at ease. Spend some time writing about what you think being authentic means. Are there times when you chose to either be authentic or not be authentic? Note those times as well.

Option #2:

Take some time this week and rewrite Acts 2:42-47 in your own words. Feel free to paraphrase the passage or rewrite it in a paragraph form. The important thing is to grasp and communicate the meaning of the passage. Be prepared to share your thoughts next week with your small group.

Bible Reference Notes

Use these notes to gain further understanding of the text as you study on your own.

Acts 2:42

The four components of the church's life here may represent what occurred at their gatherings.
teaching. The foundation for the church's life was the instruction given by the apostles as the representatives of Jesus.
fellowship. Literally, *sharing.* While this may include the aspect of sharing to meet material needs (v. 45), it most likely means their common participation in the Holy Spirit as they worshiped together (1 Cor. 12).
the breaking of bread. The Lord's Supper in which they remembered His death (Luke 22:19) and recognized His presence among them (Luke 24:30-31).
prayers. This may refer to set times and forms of prayer, as was the practice of the Jews.

Acts 2:43-47

The picture of the church is one of continual growth (v. 47) marked by generous sharing (vv. 44-45) and joyful worship and fellowship (vv. 46-47a). The worship at the temple continued as before, since the line dividing Christianity from Judaism had not yet been drawn. Christians simply saw their faith as the natural end of what the Jewish faith had always declared.

Acts 2:44

everything in common. While this may appear as a primitive form of socialism, it certainly did not include the oppressive totalitarianism or denial of God found in many modern forms. It was simply an outgrowth of the intense love people had for each other through Jesus Christ. They believed that, in Christ, each person's need becomes everyone's need.

Acts 2:47

And every day the Lord added to them. Growth in the church was a natural result of the love, fellowship, and commitment to the apostles' teaching.

Session

2 ACCEPTING ONE ANOTHER

Connections Prep

2

MAIN "LIFEPOINT": The authentic Christian community accepts others.

To reinforce the "LifePoint," leaders and small-group facilitators should understand the following more detailed CheckPoints and "Do" Points.

BIBLE STUDY CHECKPOINTS:

- Understand the need to be accepting and welcoming of others.
- Consider how we treat people based on their external appearance.
- Realize accepting people is not based on what we will get out of the relationship.

LIFE CHANGE "DO" POINTS:

- Get to know someone you would normally avoid.
- Be prepared for worship.
- Volunteer to help others during a church worship service.

PREPARATION:

- ☐ Review the leader book for this session and prepare your teaching in advance.
- ☐ Determine how you will divide students into small discussion groups.
- ☐ Recruit mature students or adults as small-group facilitators. Be sure these facilitators plan to attend your meeting.

REQUIRED SUPPLIES:

- ☐ *Contagious Community: Living Beyond Yourself* leader book for each group facilitator
- ☐ *Contagious Community: Living Beyond Yourself* student book for each student
- ☐ Pen or pencil for each student

"Get Ready" is primarily for students, but leaders and facilitators will benefit from these devotionals as well.

Get Ready

Read one of these short Bible passages each day, and spend a few minutes of focused time with God. Be sure to jot down any insights you receive.

MONDAY

Read Romans 15:7.
Who is someone in your life you have a difficult time accepting? Why is it so difficult to accept him or her? Do you pray regularly for this person? Spend some time today praying for this person.

TUESDAY

Read James 2:1-4.
Have you ever been guilty of judging someone because of the clothes they wear? Want a simple test? Look around you. Do your friends all shop at the same stores? Why do you think that is? Is there someone you used to be friends with but stopped when they weren't dressing like your personal crowd?

WEDNESDAY

Read James 2:5.
How important are material things to you? How important is it to you to be considered rich? How important is it to you to be considered rich in things of "faith"? Do your lips say one thing and your wants say something else? Spend some time today talking to God about increasing your faith without increasing your possessions.

THURSDAY

Read James 2:6-7.
What do you do when you see someone who is poor? What do you do when you pass a homeless person? Do you ever find yourself avoiding someone because of their appearance?

FRIDAY

Read James 2:8-10.
How important is it to you that you love your neighbor? Who would you say your neighbor is? Is it easier to love your neighbor or your friend? Do you love your neighbor as much as yourself? Would you say you think of yourself too much or not enough?

SATURDAY

Read James 2:11.

Why is it so difficult to keep the laws God gave us? Is it possible for you to keep each of them? Why do you think God made life so difficult? Can you do anything good for God on your own, or do you rely on His grace? When is it most difficult to rely on God?

SUNDAY

Read James 2:12-13.

Do you consider yourself merciful to those who have wronged you? Who is the person who has wronged you the most? What causes you to deserve mercy? What causes others to deserve the same mercy?

LARGE-GROUP OPENING:
Get everyone's attention. Make announcements. Open your session with a prayer. Read the "LifePoint" to students.

LifePoint

The authentic Christian community accepts others.

SMALL-GROUP TIME:
Instruct students to divide into groups of four to eight, preferably in a circle configuration.

Call on the mature student or adult leaders you recruited to facilitate each small group through this "Say What?" segment.

Say What? (15 minutes)

Random Question of the Week:

If you had one superpower, what would it be and why?

Group Experience: Fashion Choices

Share the following questions with the students in your small group and allow each student to answer. Encourage students to share their answers to the questions. The purpose of this experience is to allow students to share their thoughts with the group and also begin thinking about the groups with whom they spend their time and how they choose their friends.

1. Think about your closet. How likely are you to be wearing the latest "in" fashion?
   - ☐ I'm wearing what will be "in" style next year already.
   - ☐ Always!
   - ☐ Look at me, does it look like I could be any more "in"?
   - ☐ Sometimes, when I feel like taking the time to dress up.
   - ☐ Only on Sundays when I go to church.
   - ☐ I hate fashion. I will never be in style.
   - ☐ I have my own style and I really don't worry about what others think about it.
   - ☐ Other ______________________________

2. Think about your friends; do they have the same fashion style as you do? Why or why not?

3. What fashion style do you avoid? Do you avoid people who dress that way as well?

4. Who or what has the most influence over how you choose to dress today?

LARGE-GROUP TIME: **Direct students to turn to face the front for this teaching time. Be sure you can make eye contact with each student in the room. Encourage them to follow along and take notes in their student books.**

So What? (30 minutes)

Teaching Outline

I. Exclusivity
- A. Feeling superior
- B. Accepting differences

II. Learning from Scripture
- A. Romans 15:7
- B. James 2:1-13

III. The Right Climate
- A. Welcome one another
- B. The desire to belong

Share the "So What?" information with students. You may modify it to meet your needs. Be sure to highlight the underlined information, which gives answers to the student book questions and fill-in-the-blanks (shown in the margins).

IV. Not a Fashion Show

A. What our dress communicates

B. Emphasize relationships

V. Not a Financial Opportunity

A. Avoid showing favoritism to wealthy

B. Deny selfish interests

VI. A Community of Love and Mercy

Genuine acceptance

2

Exclusivity

❶ Why do some places make you feel unwelcome and excluded?

After the "Group Experience" ask: **Have you ever been somewhere you felt uncomfortable?** Every society has places that make you feel welcome and accepted and also places that make you feel excluded. ❶ Many places that make you feel unwelcome and excluded were created for that purpose. They were created that way to make those who were welcome feel superior to those who weren't. In New Testament times, the temple was sometimes this way. The temple excluded women from gaining access to the main part, and it also had a sign that basically warned Gentiles that attempting to enter could be hazardous to their health.

❷ What actions by church members are mentioned that convey non-acceptance of others? What are similar situations you can think of?

Today our churches are usually not as blatant with their exclusivity. Many churches however, convey subtly to outsiders they are unwelcome. Most would never admit they are exclusive, but their actions tell a different story. ❷ Imagine a student from another school coming into your church and sitting in someone's special pew. Instead of someone welcoming them, many times they are asked to move or are stared at with a menacing look. Some churches make it a point to hang a sign outside that states "All Are Welcome Here," but are quick to ignore the young man or woman who comes in not "properly dressed." ❷ Some simply turn their heads and walk away when someone with piercings, tattoos, or an unusual hair style shows up on a Sunday morning. Or maybe a person comes into a church where a demonstration of worship is raising their hands, and that person isn't comfortable raising their hands, or vice versa, maybe the person is used to raising their hands during worship but is made uncomfortable when they do so. How do others act around them then? Do they feel welcome?

❸ When a person first enters a new group or church, what question is generally on their mind?

❹ In what ways do church members' actions answer a visitor's question about belonging?

❸ The first question that people ask themselves when they walk into any place is, "Do I belong here?" Even before the first word is spoken from the stage, even before the music has begun, this person is beginning to look for answers to that question. ❹ The question is answered by the way the members talk or don't talk to them; the way members choose to smile at them or not; and by the way they are made to feel welcome and included.

Sometimes visitors stick out in a service because they don't know the words to the songs, don't look like everyone else, and they don't know what to expect next. Many times church members forget what it feels like to be on the outside looking in.

The contagious community begins when people feel welcome. Very few people are willing to jump into a new situation and be the center of attention. Most teenagers are more than willing to sit on the outside and be a wallflower while they watch the group in action. Many teenagers are willing to test the group waters more readily when they have at least one friend to go with them, but what about the students who just show up? Do they feel welcome?

Before the session, enlist youth to read Romans 15:7 and James 2:1-13.

Learning from the Bible

7 Therefore accept one another, just as the Messiah also accepted you, to the glory of God.

1 My brothers, hold your faith in our glorious Lord Jesus Christ without showing
favoritism. 2 For suppose a man comes into your meeting wearing a gold ring, dressed in
fine clothes, and a poor man dressed in dirty clothes also comes in.3 If you look with favor
on the man wearing the fine clothes so that you say, "Sit here in a good place," and yet
you say to the poor man, "Stand over there," or, "Sit here on the floor by my footstool,"
4 haven't you discriminated among yourselves and become judges with evil thoughts?
5 Listen, my dear brothers: Didn't God choose the poor in this world to be rich in
faith and heirs of the kingdom that He has promised to those who love Him? 6 Yet you
dishonored that poor man. Don't the rich oppress you and drag you into the courts?
7 Don't they blaspheme the noble name that you bear?
8 If you really carry out the royal law prescribed in Scripture, Love your neighbor as
yourself, you are doing well. 9 But if you show favoritism, you commit sin and are convicted
by the law as transgressors. 10 For whoever keeps the entire law, yet fails in one point, is
guilty of breaking it all. 11 For He who said, Do not commit adultery, also said, Do not murder.
So if you do not commit adultery, but you do murder, you are a lawbreaker.
12 Speak and act as those who will be judged by the law of freedom. 13 For judgment is
without mercy to the one who hasn't shown mercy. Mercy triumphs over judgment.

The Right Climate

Rick Warren, in his book *The Purpose-Driven Church,* states that churches who want to grow, follow Jesus' example of loving unbelievers and outsiders. He writes, "The right climate for church growth is an atmosphere of acceptance and love." While many teenagers aren't concerned about church growth, they should be concerned about the spiritual condition of others. Whether a group has 10 or 1000 in it doesn't matter to a typical teenager. What they must be concerned about is that no one misses out on the opportunity to know Jesus Christ through a contagious community that is in love with Him and His teachings.

Consider Paul of Tarsus. He called believers to model Jesus' behavior, telling them, "Therefore accept one another, just as the Messiah also accepted you, to the glory of God." (Romans 15:7). In the NRSV this is translated, "Welcome one another," which calls attention to the need of the Christian community to show a welcoming acceptance to someone from the first moment of contact, making the person feel welcomed in the midst of the community.

❺ What three things have many churches communicated to those outside the church in the past?

❻ What does the church need to communicate to those outside?

In order for someone to feel welcomed, they must not only hear that they are welcome but they must also see acceptance in the actions and interactions they have with others in the group. A smile and greeting go a long way toward making someone feel welcome, while a glance and cold shoulder go just as far in making someone feel unwelcome. When we feel welcomed into a situation it is because people accept us for who we are, not who we have the potential to become. ❺ For years many churches have told others they need to behave like we do; believe like we do; and then they will belong here. Today teenagers stay away from that mentality. The desire for belonging is important to all of us. ❻ The church today must communicate to those outside; you belong here, so you can believe what we do, and become like Christ. For many, their relationship with Christ begins with a relationship with a friend who chooses to act like Christ.

2

James urged Christians to welcome and accept people without manipulation or favoritism. His words have some important implications for what a Christian community should and should not be.

Not a Fashion Show

❼ What problem can wearing expensive clothing, jewelry, or other possessions create in a Christian fellowship?

It is important for us to realize that church or any other gathering of the Christian community is not to be a fashion show. We might think that today we don't really have to worry about that, but we do. Many Christian community gatherings are used as opportunities for people to show off their latest clothes, fashions, jewelry, and accessories. Think for a moment about Easter. How many people get new clothes for Easter? Most of us do. Why we get new clothes is the issue. We have to decide whether we are getting new clothes to look our best to honor God or if we are getting new clothes because everyone else is. It is not wrong to get new clothes or wear our best. The problem comes in when we dress in a way that brings attention to us more than to God. James refers to people who came into their fellowship wearing fine clothes and jewelry. ❼ The problem was not that they tried to look nice to honor God. The problem was that the jewelry they chose to wear (James mentions a gold ring) was a sign of status that separated them from others in their fellowship. This ring indicated they were more important than others in their midst. Also, everyone knows that certain items of clothing, whether it is the newest, coolest brand name, style, or material, are intended to communicate specific messages. Today these might be anything from the latest cell phone, the coolest car, to the hottest brand of clothes. All of these things have the effect of separating people from one another and making the less fortunate feel like second-class citizens in the fellowship.

Churches today show a lot of variety in the way they dress. Very few churches have a written dress code for their members, but the reactions, stares, and pointing that those who dress differently receive is enough to let them know what the expected dress code is. Most churches would say that the way someone dresses should not exclude them from being a part of the church, but their actions often tell a different story than their words. Some churches hold to a more traditional dress. Some churches encourage their members to dress in their "Sunday Best" to come to church. Some encourage women to wear dresses and men to wear suits. Even other churches have transitioned into more casual attire—some including jeans and T-shirts.

Many times this dress code issue makes teenagers feel like outsiders. Most teens don't wear dresses or suits to school. Many teenagers who aren't a part of a specific Christian community are unaware of what is proper to wear to an event. When they show up in what they would normally wear, others are offended and make comments. It becomes difficult for teenagers to feel like part of a community when they can't afford to dress like everyone else, especially if others put a higher emphasis on fashion than they do on a relationship with Christ. In the world, clothing often divides people, but a Christian community is called to do things a little differently from the world (John 15:19). To be an accepting community, we can not let the external element of clothing get in the way of building relationships with others.

Not a Financial Opportunity

8 Why was James confused that the church to which he was writing sometimes showed favoritism to those who were wealthy?

A community of acceptance must also be a place where people are not seen as material objects. 8 James was a bit confused at the church's frequent favoritism toward wealthy visitors since it was the wealthy who often oppressed them. The real problem however, was similar to today: people were looking at others for what might be in it for the church and the potential of getting something from someone who was wealthy. A wealthy person comes into the church and many think, *this person has it all! They could be the one to pay for our next big event, item, or video game!* Some even think on a more personal basis that the wealthy person could be a source of finance for them. Many times teenagers tend to latch onto those new students who they feel might have the latest games, technology, or the coolest clothes, simply because they think they might be able to get something from them. It is a very selfish motive but it happens in many Christian communities weekly. Unfortunately this pressure and lack of popularity is not only felt by the students who can't afford to have the most expensive things, but it also puts tremendous pressure on parents to try to provide items for their own children that they can't personally afford.

❾ In what way does showing favoritism toward the wealthy dishonor both the rich and the poor?

❾ Equating wealthy people to financial opportunity and material things dishonors both the rich and the poor, as well as those in between. It dishonors those who can't afford the most expensive items because it communicates a diminished importance within the community. This dishonors the wealthy since it clouds the ability to really see their soul and who God created them at their core. It also gives many wealthy people a distorted view of God—one that tells them that God loves them more if they have more "things." Today, we might not force someone who is poor to sit in an unfavorable place, but we do often overlook them, ignore them, and pay them less attention while attempting to get to know a wealthier person.

A Community of Love and Mercy

In order for us to become Christian communities who care about each other and accept each other, we need to focus beyond the list of things not to do. We also need to pay attention to what we do. We not only need to treat everyone equally, by not showing favoritism, but we also must show all people love and mercy. James states, "Love your neighbor as yourself," (v. 8), and he calls us to show mercy to each other (v. 13). If we choose to treat everyone the same and withhold love and mercy, we do not become a contagious community. ❿ Mercy and acceptance are very closely related. Mercy means not rejecting someone because of what they have done wrong or what they have failed at. God shows us mercy in offering us salvation even when we sin (Romans 5:8). We need to consciously show that same mercy to each other, both those inside and outside our Christian communities. Mercy is shown when we accept others even through their faults, rather than criticizing them for their failures.

❿ What is "mercy," and how can we show it?

People today hunger to be accepted. Think about your own life. When you go into a new situation you long to be accepted rather than be an outsider. The acceptance people search for today goes into the external showing of our fashions and the internal of our lives. Acceptance is genuinely felt when someone is included regardless of his or her dress or past failures. A Christian community should be a place where people can go to get this hunger filled.

SMALL-GROUP TIME: After presenting the teaching material, ask students to divide back into small groups and discuss the "Do What?" questions. Small-group facilitators should lead the discussions and set the model for being open and honest in responding to questions.

Do What? (15 minutes)

Making It Personal

1. What kind of person is least likely to feel welcomed and accepted when he or she comes into your life? into your school? into your Christian community?

2. What does James say happens to us when we show favoritism? Why do you think it is so difficult not to show favoritism? Do you struggle with showing favoritism?

3. In which of the following ways do you find yourself showing an unfair or unloving kind of favoritism? Mark as many ways as apply to you:
   - ☐ I tend to show a preference to people who are wealthier than I am.
   - ☐ I have a prejudice against people who are wealthier than I am.
   - ☐ I prefer to be around good looking (attractive) people.
   - ☐ I have a preference against certain (or other) races.
   - ☐ I avoid older people.
   - ☐ I avoid younger kids.
   - ☐ I have a prejudice against people who aren't from where I am from.
   - ☐ I show a preference to people who are like me.
   - ☐ Other ______________________________

4. Can you think of a time when favoritism would be the right thing?

Small-group facilitators should reinforce the "LifePoint" for this session, making sure that students' questions are invited and addressed honestly.

LifePoint Review

The authentic Christian community accepts others.

"Do" Points

These "Do" Points will help you begin to experience this week's "LifePoint." Be open and honest as you discuss the action points within your small group.

1. Get to know someone you would normally avoid. This might mean you take the time to get to know someone you have a prejudice against or going out of your way not to show a preference to people just like you. Ask someone who isn't one of your "usual" friends to sit with you at lunch, ride to school with you, grab a bite to eat with you, or invite them to church with you.

2. Be prepared for worship. Next time you head to church, before you go out the door, take a few minutes and look at the way you are dressed. How are you dressed and why are you dressed that way? Are you hoping to impress someone with the way you are dressed or are you hoping someone might notice the name brand of your clothes? If you normally dress slouchy, take a few extra minutes and dress up. If you normally are dressed up, try jeans and a T-shirt. How are you treated by others when you don't look like you normally do? Do people even notice? Do people talk? What can you learn from this that helps you treat others differently?

3. Volunteer to help others during a church worship service. What would happen if you stood outside the doors of your church and greeted everyone the same way on a Sunday morning? Try greeting everyone the same way. Greet children, teenagers, and adults the same. See what happens when you shake the hand of the person who can't afford the nicest clothes with the same excitement you shake the hands of the wealthiest family in the church. What happens to people when you treat them this way?

Encourage students to list prayer needs for others in their books so they can pray for one another during the week.

Assign a student coordinator in each small group to gather the group's requests and e-mail them to the group members.

Prayer Connection:

This is the time to encourage, support, and pray for each other in our journeys to trust God and seek out real and personal encounters with Him.

Share prayer needs and requests with the group, especially those related to hearing from and responding to God. Your group facilitator will close your time in prayer.

Prayer Needs:

Encourage students to dig a little deeper by completing a "Now What?" assignment before the next time you meet.

Remind students about the "Get Ready" short daily Bible readings and related questions at the beginning of session 3.

Now What?

Deepen your understanding of who God is and His desire for us to have an authentic Christian community, and continue the journey you've begun today by choosing one of the following assignments to complete this week:

Option #1:
If you enjoy writing, take the time this week to keep a journal about the times you spend with others. Notice how you interact with others and note if you observe a difference in the way you and your friends treat each other and those outside your circle of friends. Note how you feel when you see certain people. Note the people who are easy to accept and those who are more difficult to be around. Spend time daily praying for both those who are easy to accept and those who aren't.

Option #2:
Take some time this week and rewrite James 2:1-13 in your own words. Feel free to paraphrase the passage or rewrite it in paragraph form. The important thing is to grasp and communicate the meaning of the passage. Be prepared to share your thoughts next week with your small group.

Bible Reference Notes

Use these notes to gain further understanding of the text as you study on your own.

Romans 15:7

as the Messiah also accepted you. Jesus did not make us live up to some artificial standard before loving us and dying for us. As the old hymn states, He let each of us come "just as I am, without one plea."
to the glory of God. God is glorified by our acceptance of each other because it reflects His own love, which is not based on externals.

James 2:2

a gold ring. This was the mark of those who belonged to the equestrian order—the second level of Roman aristocracy. These noblemen were typically wealthy. Rings (in general) were a sign of wealth. Early Christians were urged to wear only one ring, on the little finger, bearing the image of a dove, fish, or anchor.
fine clothes. These are literally *bright and shining* garments, like those worn by the angels in Acts 10:30.
poor man. The word used here denotes a beggar, a person from the lowest level of society.
dirty clothes. In contrast to the spotless garments of the rich man, the beggar wears filthy rags, probably because this is all he owns. Our treatment of others should not be based on outward appearances.

James 2:5

rich in faith and heirs of the kingdom. James often echoes Jesus' teachings, and this is one example. In Luke's version of the Beatitudes, Jesus said, "Blessed are you who are poor, because the kingdom of God is yours" (Luke 6:20).

James 2:6

oppress you. In a day of abject poverty, the poor were often forced to borrow money at exorbitant rates of interest just to survive. The rich profited from their need.
drag you into the courts. This was probably over the issue of a debt.

James 2:7

the noble name. The early followers of Jesus were dubbed with the name "Christians" (Acts 11:26). At baptism they formally took upon themselves the name of Christ, knowing that they might well be vilified simply for bearing that name.

James 2:8

the royal law. This phrase recognizes that Jesus exalted this law as one of the two greatest commandments.

James 2:12

the law of freedom. Judaism had become encrusted with countless rules that bound people. Christians had only one principle to follow: to love others freely as Christ loved them (1:25; 2:8).

Notes

Session 3

LOVING ONE ANOTHER

Connections Prep

3

MAIN "LIFEPOINT": As we pour out love to others through our actions, we represent God.

To reinforce the "LifePoint," leaders and small-group facilitators should understand the following more detailed CheckPoints and "Do" Points.

BIBLE STUDY CHECKPOINTS:

- Consider what it means to love another person from a biblical perspective.
- Understand how real love needs to be shown through actions.
- See how loving others relates to our status with God.

LIFE CHANGE "DO" POINTS:

- Perform an act of love for someone for whom you have previously felt no love.
- Donate to a ministry that helps others.
- Pray for someone in your church who is sick or homebound.

PREPARATION:

- ☐ Review the leader book for this session and prepare your teaching in advance.
- ☐ Determine how you will divide students into small discussion groups.
- ☐ Recruit mature students or adults as small-group facilitators. Be sure these facilitators plan to attend your meeting.

REQUIRED SUPPLIES:

- ☐ *Contagious Community: Living Beyond Yourself* leader book for each group facilitator
- ☐ *Contagious Community: Living Beyond Yourself* student book for each student
- ☐ Pen or pencil for each student

"Get Ready" is primarily for students, but leaders and facilitators will benefit from these devotionals as well.

Get Ready

Read one of these short Bible passages each day, and spend a few minutes of focused time with God. Be sure to jot down any insights you receive.

MONDAY

Read 1 John 3:11-12.
Is it easier to act out of jealousy or love? Why? When have you chosen to act out of jealousy rather than love recently?

TUESDAY

Read 1 John 3:13.
Have you ever experienced the "hate" of the world? Why? How does being rejected by the world make you feel? Why?

WEDNESDAY

Read 1 John 3:14-15.
How real is hate to you? Have you ever been hated? What for? Have you ever hated someone else? Why? How do you deal with hate?

THURSDAY

Read 1 John 3:16.
What does love look like to you? When was the last time you chose to give up something that was important to you? Why did you decide to give it up?

FRIDAY

Read 1 John 3:17-18.
Do you believe God's love can be shown to others? Do you believe you can show that love to others? How are you demonstrating God's love on a regular basis? Why?

SATURDAY

Read 1 John 3:19-20.

When was the last time you felt guilty for something? Could guilt be something that God gives us to keep us close to Him? How do you deal with your guilt? What helps you set your guilt at ease?

SUNDAY

Read 1 John 3:21-24.

How important is it for you to feel loved by someone else? How important is it for you to be loved by someone else? How does it affect your relationship with God when you act in love toward someone else?

3

LARGE-GROUP OPENING:
Get everyone's attention. Make announcements. Open your session with a prayer. Read the "LifePoint" to students.

LifePoint

As we pour out love to others through our actions, we represent God.

SMALL-GROUP TIME:
Instruct students to divide into groups of four to eight, preferably in a circle configuration.

Call on the mature student or adult leaders you recruited to facilitate each small group through this "Say What?" segment.

Say What? (15 minutes)

Random Question of the Week:

If you were a food, what would you be and why?

Group Experience: "Love" Questions

Share the following "love" questions with the students in your small group and allow each student to answer. Encourage students to share their answers to the questions. The purpose of this experience is to allow students to share their thoughts with the group and also begin thinking about the groups with whom they spend their time.

1. Who is the person you find yourself competing with the most? Who is your biggest rival?
   - ☐ A brother or sister
   - ☐ Another family member
   - ☐ a friend who is just like a brother or sister to me
   - ☐ Someone who always criticizes me
   - ☐ A parent (or relative) who appears to have always done things well when they were my age
   - ☐ Rivals? I don't have rivals and I don't compete with anyone else.
   - ☐ Other ______________________________

2. In what area of your life does competition or rivalry most affect you? Why?

3. How do you feel when you are around the person you consider to be your rival?

LARGE-GROUP TIME: **Direct students to turn to face the front for this teaching time. Be sure you can make eye contact with each student in the room. Encourage them to follow along and take notes in their student books.**

Share the "So What?" information with students. You may modify it to meet your needs. Be sure to highlight the underlined information, which gives answers to the student book questions and fill-in-the-blanks (shown in the margins).

So What? (30 minutes)

Teaching Outline

I. The Need for Love

A. Loving our neighbor

B. True love versus sexual love

C. Jesus' definition of love

II. Learning from the Bible

1 John 3:11-24

III. Love Defined

A. Romantic physical love

B. Brotherly love

C. Self-giving, unconditional love

IV. A Sign of Our Faith

How we love others

V. Shown in Action

More than talk

VI. A Clear Conscience

A. Believe in Jesus

B. Love one another

The Need for Love

❶ What early Old Testament passage calls us to love our neighbor?

❷ What problems arise when we define love as something sexual or as a feeling?

❸ How has Jesus defined love for us through His actions?

After the "Group Experience" ask: **What do you think of when you hear the word "love"?** You might agree with the words of songs that state "love is a wonderful thing," or "all you need is love." The Christian and secular world both seem to agree that the world needs more love. ❶ The desire for love has been around for ages. The Bible discusses the need for us to love our neighbor as early as Leviticus 19:18. Jesus mentions loving others only after He encourages us to love the Lord, and John strongly recommends that we "love another" (John 3:11). First John, one of the shortest books in the Bible, uses the word "love" over 30 times. The message of love is one that we are very familiar with, both inside the church and in the world outside.

While both the world and the church would agree we need more love, we don't seem to agree on how to define it. ❷ Many in the secular world want to define love as something sexual or as a mere feeling, but this definition of love has no strength. This definition is fickle and fleeting and very temporary. In fact, this definition lends people to believe that they can fall in and out of love quickly and often. When love is described as something only physical, unreliable, and less than profound, the result is conflict and pain.

John gives us a more dependable way of understanding love. He writes, "This is how we have come to know love: He laid down His life for us" (1 John 3:16). ❸ Jesus gives us a true definition and explanation of love. His love was not something that was out to serve Himself, but He brought a love that taught the giving away of ourselves and His offer of eternal life through His life. He was self-giving in ministering to the needs of hurting people, and He was self-giving in offering His life on the cross to atone for our sin. Imitating this kind of love does not result in pain and relationships littered with wounds, but true community. True, authentic community is something the world longs for now. People seek out others who will accept and love them. Take a look at someone's yard the next time you drive by. Are people there? Are they interacting with others? Does your family interact with your neighbors?

The Christian community reflects the love that Jesus modeled for us when we embrace people and love one another regardless of the situation.

Before the session, enlist a youth to read 1 John 3:11-24.

Learning from the Bible

11 For this is the message you have heard from the beginning: we should love one another, 12 unlike Cain, who was of the evil one and murdered his brother. And why did he murder him? Because his works were evil, and his brother's were righteous. 13 Do not be surprised, brothers, if the world hates you. 14 We know that we have passed from death to life because we love our brothers. The one who does not love remains in death. 15 Everyone who hates his brother is a murderer, and you know that no murderer has eternal life residing in him.

16 This is how we have come to know love: He laid down His life for us. We should also lay down our lives for our brothers. 17 If anyone has this world's goods and sees his brother in need but shuts off his compassion from him—how can God's love reside in him?

18 Little children, we must not love in word or speech, but in deed and truth; 19 that is how we will know we are of the truth, and will convince our hearts in His presence, 20 because if our hearts condemn us, God is greater than our hearts and knows all things.

21 Dear friends, if our hearts do not condemn us we have confidence before God, 22 and can receive whatever we ask from Him because we keep His commands and do what is pleasing in His sight. 23 Now this is his command: that we believe in the name of His Son Jesus Christ, and love one another as He commanded us. 24 The one who keeps His commands remains in Him, and He in him. And the way we know that He remains in us is from the Spirit He has given us.

Love Defined

❹ What are the three Greek words used for "love" in the New Testament, and what do they mean?

Somehow love has lost its meaning since the days of Christ. Love songs today have become a section in music stores, love stories are playing on television and the big movie screen, while classics such as *Casablanca* and *Gone with the Wind* are still around. The word "love" today is something that could mean many things. We use the same word, "love," to describe how we feel about our parents, our friends, our car, our favorite food, and our pets! ❹ In the Greek language love is described in three words; *eros,* which means *a romantic physical love; philios,* which means *brotherly love;* and *agape,* which means *self-giving love that is unconditional.* Today society and culture have twisted the meaning of love to be a self-serving romantic love that is temporary, while God's intention for love as a self-giving action is being lost.

While romantic love is obviously God-given and vital to the world, there needs to be more emphasis on showing the *philios* and *agape* love to one another. Romantic love has the potential to bring division and rivalry, but love that is *philios,* or even better, *agape,* is the cornerstone of a close-knit Christian community. *Philios* is love with which people in the Christian community support and affirm each other in difficult times. It is when people give each other a call just to check on one another. It is

❺ What is special about *agape* love?

when they take the time to lift up someone else in prayer. *Agape* love is shown when people go "beyond the call of duty" and truly sacrifice for others in a way that is both unconditional and unexpected. ❺ *Agape* love is a love that expects nothing in return and is given freely, even to those who don't want it. This is the showing of God's forgiveness and mercy. *Agape* love is fully giving ourselves away to someone else. It is impossible to express *agape* love to a car or food!

John gives us some important instructions on how to achieve a community-building love and what that can mean for us.

A Sign of Our Faith

❻ What does John refer to as a sure indicator of faith?

❻ John wrote that community-building love (*philios* and *agape* love) is a sure indicator of faith. Verse 14 reads, "We know that we have passed from death to life because we love our brothers. The one who does not love remains in death." John also wrote in verse 19, that showing this kind of love is "how we will know we are of the truth." The most crucial part of our faith is not our knowledge of the Bible (as important as this is); it is not how well we can argue with others about our faith; it is not our attendance in a Christian community; rather, the most crucial part is shown in how we love others.

Consider what the Apostle Paul wrote about love in 1 Corinthians 13:1-3:

> ***If I speak the languages of men and of angels, but do not have love,***
> ***I am a sounding gong or a clanging cymbal.***
> ***If I have the gift of prophecy,***
> ***and understand all mysteries and all knowledge,***
> ***and if I have all faith, so that I can move mountains,***
> ***but do not have love, I am nothing.***
> ***And if I donate all my goods to feed the poor,***
> ***and if I give my body to be burned,***
> ***but do not have love, I gain nothing.***

Paul continued in this chapter to exalt love over even "faith" and "hope." This "love" chapter might be familiar as part of a wedding ceremony, but it is not reserved for couples on their wedding day! This love that Paul describes is intended for everyone to experience.

Shown in Action

John also wrote that love has to be shown through our actions. Verse 18 states very clearly, "Little children we must not love in word or speech, but in deed and truth." When John gives these instructions, he is in solid agreement with the teaching of Jesus. Other early Christian leaders echo this teaching as well. ❼ Jesus said, "Not

7 Besides John, what two other New Testament teachers emphasized that love has to be shown in action?

everyone who says to Me, 'Lord, Lord!' will enter the kingdom of heaven, but only the one who does the will of My Father in heaven" (Matt. 7:21). And James declared, "But be doers of the word and not hearers only, deceiving yourselves" (Jas. 1:22). James also gave a specific example of the need for action when he wrote, "If a brother or sister is without clothes and lacks daily food, and one of you says to them, 'Go in peace, keep warm, and eat well,' but you don't give them what the body needs, what good is it? In the same way faith, if it doesn't have works, is dead by itself" (Jas. 2:15-17). This is very similar to what John wrote in verse 17, "If anyone has this world's goods and sees his brother in need but shuts off his compassion from him—how can God's love reside in him?"

8 What are three ways to show love in action to someone in emotional or spiritual need?

Love must be shown in our actions. This will not always mean sharing our possessions with the physically needy. 8 Sometimes we must share willingly with those who are spiritually and emotionally needy. It means lending a listening ear to a person who is depressed or hurting. It means being real and genuine and faithful in our conversations with others, and in praying for someone else's needs. It means following through to help that person find the resources they need for his or her problem, even going the extra mile and getting them help you might not feel comfortable giving them. You might even need to look out for someone's best interest by going with them to seek counseling, talking to a trusted adult, or going with them to talk to a friend with whom they need to restore a relationship.

Confidence and trust are built when love is evident through our actions. An evident love helps build a contagious Christian community. People want to be a part of a Christian community that is about more than just talking about love. People want to be a part of a love that is active in relationships with others both inside and outside the community.

The Path to a Clear Conscience

When we choose to show others love, it not only helps them see the need and validity of our Christian community, but it also plays a role in finding the path to a clear conscience before God. John says if we genuinely love others, "we will know we are of the truth, and will convince our hearts in His presence, because if our hearts condemn us, God is greater than our hearts and knows all things" (vv. 19-20). God really knows and sees what is in our hearts more than we may realize. John concluded this thought by writing, "Dear friends, if our hearts do not condemn us we have confidence before God" (v. 21). So we can rest in knowing that God really does know and care about us and when He lives in us we can trust our hearts. We will know when our conscience is experiencing guilt and we will know when we are clean before Him.

When we have a guilty conscience, we find that it might be very difficult to find relief. John even tells us we will experience times when our hearts condemn us, but we just remember that God is greater than our hearts. John was saying that if we follow God's commandment to love and do it in a genuine way through action, then at least we have some ammunition to use in answering our consciences. John also points to another component vital to a clear conscience: faith in Jesus Christ.

❾ What are two important elements in having a clear conscience before God?

❾ Two commandments become essential. John wrote in verse 23, "Now this is His command: that we believe in the name of His Son Jesus Christ, and love one another as He commanded us." John is telling us, "Believe in the love God showed you in sending His Son to die for your sin, and believe in His command to emulate that love by loving each other." When we follow both of these commands, a guilty conscience has no room in our lives.

SMALL-GROUP TIME: Use this time to help students begin to integrate the truth they've learned into their lives while they connect with other students in the group, the leaders, and with God.

After presenting the teaching material, ask students to divide back into small groups and discuss the "Do What?" questions. Small-group facilitators should lead the discussions and set the model for being open and honest in responding to questions.

Do What? (15 minutes)

Making It Personal

1. What does Jesus' sacrifice of His life on the cross tell us about the nature of love? (v. 16)

2. After reading verses 19-21, what would you say is the connection between a guilty conscience (where your "heart condemns you") and how God feels toward you? What is John saying that a person with a guilty conscience should do?

3. What is the hardest teaching in this passage for you to follow?
   - ☐ Loving my own family; I can really relate to Cain (vv. 11-12)
   - ☐ Feeling like not everyone likes me (v. 13)
   - ☐ Learning to deal with the hate and anger I have toward certain people (vv. 14-15)
   - ☐ Realizing that Jesus is calling me to sacrifice myself like He did (v. 16)
   - ☐ Choosing to lay down my life and loving others sacrificially (v. 16)
   - ☐ Sharing my stuff (v. 17)
   - ☐ Dealing with my own guilt (vv. 19-21)
   - ☐ Focusing on pleasing God over choosing to please myself (v. 22)
   - ☐ Realizing that God really lives in me and being confident of it (v. 24)
   - ☐ Other ________________________________

Complete this sentence: I could show someone God's love today by . . .

Small-group facilitators should reinforce the "LifePoint" for this session, making sure that students' questions are invited and addressed honestly.

LifePoint Review

As we pour out love to others through our actions, we represent God.

"Do" Points

These "Do" Points will help you begin to experience this week's "LifePoint." Be open and honest as you discuss the action points within your small group.

1. Perform an act of love for someone for whom you have previously felt no love. Don't wait until you feel like loving someone to show them love. Start just by doing a loving act. This might mean letting them know you are praying for them during a difficult time, offering to help them study for a test, inviting them to sit with you at lunch, or simply calling them to see how they are doing. As a teenager, stepping out into a loving act puts you in the most vulnerable position imaginable and makes you susceptible to ridicule or embarrassment, but with God watching your back, what do you have to lose? If the person never changes the way he or she looks at you, you have lost nothing, rather you have gained the knowledge of your doing something for Christ, without expecting something kind in return. It's the beginning steps of becoming like Christ.

2. Donate to a ministry that helps others. Give up something that means a great deal to you. That might mean giving up your gourmet coffee for a month and donating that money to help others. Maybe you will sell something you care about or even hold off on buying something so you can give that money away. Give away more than your spare change. Make sure the ministry you give your money to is a reputable ministry, where donations go directly to meet the needs of others rather than to administrative fees and salaries.

3. Pray for someone in your church who is sick or homebound. Check with your church to see if they have a list of those in the hospital who have a long-term illness or are homebound. Most churches have these lists. Don't just call them up or visit them and tell them you are praying for them, actually do it! Take the time to pray for them when you see them and when you are away from them. That is part of loving in "truth and deed" instead of just using your words.

Encourage students to list prayer needs for others in their books so they can pray for one another during the week.

Assign a student coordinator in each small group to gather the group's requests and e-mail them to the group members.

Prayer Connection:

This is the time to encourage, support, and pray for each other in our journeys to trust God and seek out real and personal encounters with Him.

Share prayer needs and requests with the group, especially those related to hearing from and responding to God. Your group facilitator will close your time in prayer.

Prayer Needs:

Encourage students to dig a little deeper by completing a "Now What?" assignment before the next time you meet.

Remind students about the "Get Ready" daily Bible readings and related questions at the beginning of session 4.

Now What?

Remind them again this week that they are loved!

Deepen your understanding of who God is and His desire for us to have an authentic Christian community, and continue the journey you've begun today by choosing one of the following assignments to complete this week:

Option #1:

If you enjoy writing, take the time this week to keep a journal about the times when you notice yourself either choosing to love like Christ or withhold it from someone else. Note how you feel when you notice that you are willingly loving someone. Do you just love someone who deserves it? Do you find yourself loving someone without them loving you back? Are you withholding your love from someone because you need to deal with sin in your own life? Take care to note times when God leads you to love someone you normally wouldn't.

Option #2:

Take some time this week and rewrite 1 John 3:11-24 in your own words. Feel free to paraphrase the passage or rewrite it in paragraph form. The important thing is to grasp and communicate the meaning of the passage. Be prepared to share your thoughts next week with your small group.

Bible Reference Notes

Use these notes to gain further understanding of the text as you study on your own:

1 John 3:11

this is the message. In 1:5, John used this same phrase to introduce the great truth that lies at the heart of the Christian message: God is light. Here he uses this phrase to introduce a second core insight: love is at the center of the Christian life.

1 John 3:12

And why did he murder him? Cain became jealous because God seemed to prefer Abel's offering to his own. The evil came in this reaction of jealousy, which led Cain to murder his brother (Gen. 4:1-16).

1 John 3:15

hates his brother is a murderer. Jesus took the law against murder and raised the ante, saying that even those who have hate in their hearts against their brother or sister are like murderers (Matt. 5:21-22).

no murderer has eternal life. This is not a denial of grace. A murderer forgiven by the grace of God in Jesus Christ is no longer a murderer from the divine perspective.

1 John 3:16-17

John next offers a positive example of love: Jesus' sacrificial love for the human race. Both the example of Cain and the example of Jesus involve death. But Cain's act sprang from hatred and took the life of another, while Jesus' act sprang from love and He gave His own life for others.

1 John 3:19-20

John seems to be saying that Christians can be secure in their relationship with God even when their consciences trouble them. The basis of their confidence is the fact that it is God who will judge them and not their own hearts. They can trust themselves to His all-knowing justice because they have loved as He commanded (v. 18), and because they have sought and found His forgiveness (1 Cor. 4:3-5).

1 John 3:21

confidence. Confidence is necessary in order to come before God. Without confidence a person is held back by feelings of unworthiness. Hebrews 4:16 tells us, "Therefore let us approach the throne of grace with boldness, so that we may receive mercy and find grace to help us at the proper time."

1 John 3:22

Once again, John states a truth in a stark, unqualified way: if we ask, we will receive.

keep His commands. Obedience to God's commands is not the cause of answered prayer; it is the condition that motivates Christians to pray.

1 John 3:23-24

In these verses, John brings together the three issues that underlie the three tests by which believers can know they are truly children of God. He shows the interconnection between obedience (the moral test), love (the social test), and belief (the faith test) and how these relate to the question of union with God.

Session

9 BEING PATIENT WITH EACH OTHER

Connections Prep

MAIN "LIFEPOINT": Patience develops with time and cannot be rushed.

To reinforce the "LifePoint," leaders and small-group facilitators should understand the following more detailed CheckPoints and "Do" Points.

BIBLE STUDY CHECKPOINTS:

- Understand the importance of being patient with one another when developing a contagious community.
- Become more patient with others because God is patient with us.
- See the relationship between patience and submission.

LIFE CHANGE "DO" POINTS:

- Write a "Letter to Philemon" to yourself, calling for patience with someone with whom you are being impatient.
- Perform an assessment of the role that the patience of others has played in your life.
- Be an advocate for patience this week in the life of someone else.

PREPARATION:

- ☐ Review the leader book for this session and prepare your teaching in advance.
- ☐ Determine how you will divide students into small discussion groups.
- ☐ Recruit mature students or adults as small-group facilitators. Be sure these facilitators plan to attend your meeting.

REQUIRED SUPPLIES:

- ☐ *Contagious Community: Living Beyond Yourself* leader book for each group facilitator
- ☐ *Contagious Community: Living Beyond Yourself* student book for each student
- ☐ Pen or pencil for each student

"Get Ready" is primarily for students, but leaders and facilitators will benefit from these devotionals as well.

Get Ready

Read one of these short Bible passages each day, and spend a few minutes of focused time with God. Be sure to jot down any insights you receive.

MONDAY

Read Ephesians 4:1-2.

Who tries your patience the most? How? How do you react to someone who tries your patience? How could you show Christ's love to that person today?

TUESDAY

Read Ephesians 4:3.

Do you sense a feeling of unity with other believers now? If so, why? If not, why not? How important is unity with others to you? How does unity with other believers impact those around you?

WEDNESDAY

Read Philemon 8-10.

How do you react when someone tries to force you to do something? Is someone pressuring you to be a part of something you know you should be doing on your own? How do you feel when someone points out something you know needs to be done that you are not doing?

THURSDAY

Read Philemon 11-13.

Whose help and support are you relying on right now? Who is your biggest encourager? Have you told this person how important he or she is to you? How could you tell them how important they are to you?

FRIDAY

Read Philemon 14-16.

Whom do you know who is like a brother or sister to you? How did that relationship begin and what caused it to be so important?

SATURDAY

Read Philemon 17-19.

Have you ever willingly taken on someone else's burdens or debts? How could you take on someone else's burdens or debts this week? How would an act like that help you understand what Christ has done for you?

SUNDAY

Read Philemon 20-21.

Is it difficult for you to ask for someone's help in a situation? When is it easier to ask for help? When is it more difficult to ask for help? In what way does asking someone for help bring your relationship closer together?

LARGE-GROUP OPENING:

Get everyone's attention. Make announcements. Open your session with a prayer. Read the "LifePoint" to students.

LifePoint

Patience develops with time and cannot be rushed.

SMALL-GROUP TIME: Instruct students to divide into groups of four to eight, preferably in a circle configuration.

Call on the mature student or adult leaders you recruited to facilitate each small group through this "Say What?" segment.

Say What? (15 minutes)

Random Question of the Week:

If you could travel in time, where would you go and why?

Group Experience: "Patience" Questions

Share the following "patience" questions with the students in your small group and allow each student to answer. Encourage students to share their answers to the questions. The purpose of this experience is to allow students to share their thoughts with the group and also begin thinking about the groups with whom they spend their time.

1. Which of the following do you have a hard time waiting for?
   - ☐ Christmas
   - ☐ Summer vacation
   - ☐ My birthday
   - ☐ My driver's license
   - ☐ Being able to move out on my own
   - ☐ Turning 18
   - ☐ Being old enough to date
   - ☐ Other ______________________

2. When someone is late and makes you wait on them, how do you react? Have you ever been late? How do people react to you when they have to wait on you?

3. Do you have a problem with making people wait on a regular basis? When you are late, what do your friends say? Do they expect you to be late or are they concerned about you because you are never late? How does your being on time show respect for other's time?

LARGE-GROUP TIME: Direct students to turn to face the front for this teaching time. Be sure you can make eye contact with each student in the room. Encourage them to follow along and take notes in their student books.

Share the "So What?" information with students. You may modify it to meet your needs. Be sure to highlight the underlined information, which gives answers to the student book questions and fill-in-the-blanks (shown in the margins).

So What? (30 minutes)

Teaching Outline

I. Instant Gratification
- A. Develop patience

II. Learning from the Bible
- A. Ephesians 4:1-3
- B. Philemon 8-21

III. Examples of Patience
- A. Real-life church situations
- B. Paul and Onesimus

IV. Patience and Worth
Gaining a brother or sister

V. Patience and Submission
Our submission to God

VI. Patience and Unity
Team work

Instant Gratification

❶ What are some situations in which we are used to everything being instant when it hasn't always been that way?

After the "Group Experience" say: **Lord, give me patience and give it to me now!** Point out that the ironic part of that statement is that we can't even be patient in getting the very thing we're asking for: patience. Today we live in a world in which patience is almost non-existence. ❶ <u>Today we are used to instant gratification—we don't have to wait on anything. In the past, dinner might have taken hours to get ready. Today we can thaw, heat, cook, and/or reheat a meal with the microwave in a matter of minutes. In the past, in order to research a particular topic, we (or our parents) had to go to the library, find our books in the card catalog, find the books, look up the relevant information in a book, take notes, and repeat for each book we found on the subject. Today, however, we can type in our topic on an Internet search engine and have possibly millions of results from all over the world in a matter of seconds. If that process takes minutes instead of seconds, we tend to</u>

complain about our slow computer. Finally, in the past, we had to wait for weeks as we exchanged letters by mail. We waited anxiously for a reply. Today we can instantly talk to our friends across the world by e-mail and instant message on our computer, or we can "text message" our friends when we don't have any more minutes left on our cell phone. The latest big movie can present and solve the world's largest problems in less than two hours. If that is too slow, we can always fast forward through the boring parts.

The problem with everything being available at our fingertips is that people are still people. We don't have a reset button like the latest video games do, we can't fast forward our lives through the boring or tough parts, and we don't have a delete button that allows us to get rid of things we don't like. It's hard to be patient with people when we live in an "instant" society.

❷ What is the implication of the statement "God isn't finished with us yet"?

❸ What four biblical passages are mentioned that call us to patience?

We must however learn to develop patience with one another. Patience is a key part of the contagious Christian community. Like all living things, humans need patience to grow and mature. How good does it do to scream at a seed? Does it grow faster if we yell at it? No; neither do humans. We do not react well to others' impatience with us. Another popular saying is, "Have patience with me; God isn't finished with me yet!" This statement is very true. ❷ God isn't finished with any of us yet. Daily He adds to and molds us as His creations. We cannot give up on anyone because God is continually working on him or her. No one has attained perfection here on earth, but we must continue to strive for it. We will see Him change us over time, not instantly, as He molds and shapes us. The Bible speaks in many places about the need for us to be patient with others. ❸ In Ephesians 4:1-2, we are instructed "to walk . . . with patience." In 1 Corinthians 13:4, we are told to aspire to love and that "love is patient"; in 1 Thessalonians 5:14, we are instructed to "be patient with everyone." Galatians 5:22 informs us that patience is a fruit of the Spirit.

Before the session, enlist youth to read Ephesians 4:1-3 and Philemon 8-21.

Learning from the Bible

1 I, therefore, the prisoner in the Lord, urge you to walk worthy of the calling you have received, 2 with all humility and gentleness, with patience, accepting one another in love, 3 diligently keeping the unity of the Spirit with the peace that binds us.

8 For this reason, although I have great boldness in Christ to command you to do what is right, 9 I appeal, instead, on the basis of love. I , Paul, as an elderly man and now also as a prisoner of Christ Jesus, 10 appeal to you for my child, whom I fathered while in chains—Onesimus. 11 Once he was useless to you, but now he is useful to both you and me. 12 I am sending him—a part of myself—back to you. 13 I wanted to keep him with me, so that in my imprisonment for the gospel he might serve me in your place. 14 But

I didn't want to do anything without your consent, so that your good deed might not be out of obligation, but of your own free will. [15] ***For perhaps this is why he was separated from you for a brief time, so that you might get back permanently,*** [16] ***no longer as a slave, but more than a slave—as a dearly loved brother. This is especially so to me, but even more to you, both in the flesh and in the Lord.***

[17] ***So if you consider me a partner, accept him as you would me.*** [18] ***And if he has wronged you in any way, or owes you anything, charge that to my account.*** [19] ***I, Paul, write this with my own hand: I will repay it—not to mention to you that you owe me even your own self.*** [20] ***Yes, brother, may I have joy from you in the Lord; refresh my heart in Christ.*** [21] ***Since I am confident of your obedience, I am writing to you, knowing that you will do even more than I say.***

Examples of Patience

❹ In what real-life church situations is patience especially needed?

How important is patience to the contagious community? We must look at some modern-day examples, as well as by looking at the scriptural example of Philemon and Onesimus. ❹ First, we will look at three examples from real-life church situations. Contagious community requires that we learn to be patient with people of different ages, with different leadership styles, and with those at different levels of spiritual maturity than ourselves.

As a teenager, you must realize the importance of being patient with those who are older than you. Many times an older person takes the time to think through the process they are in or the situation they are going through, taking the time to draw from their past experiences. This may even cause them to move at a slower pace than you desire to move. This, many times, irritates a younger adrenaline-driven teenager who desires to do everything quickly and without delay.

In a Christian community, we need to be patient with different styles of leadership. In most cases, church leaders themselves are learning to work with the volunteers involved in the ministries. Some churches have staff members who are full time and trained in biblical leadership skills, while other churches might have volunteer leaders who work from their own business training. As teenagers, you must learn to work alongside the leaders of ministry. The church community must develop a patient mentality of learning to work together. In the Christian community the "my way or the highway" philosophy is impossible in anything other than biblical mandates. God is the only One with ultimate authority. As humans, we must learn to work together.

Finally, we are all at different levels of spiritual maturity. We must learn that while we are extremely interested in learning how to grow in a relationship with Christ, others might not see the need in it. While you might be struggling to spend time daily with God reading His Word, another person might be struggling to change their language or even trust Him. "Patience," in this setting, is us learning to exist together and "promote love and good works" (Hebrews 10:24). By getting behind each other, we promote patience in the contagious Christian community.

We must understand what patience means as we work with real people in the church. In Philemon, Paul was trying to do this. He was trying to help someone understand what it means to be patient with another human being who makes mistakes. He was writing to Philemon, a Christian slave owner, about the need to give his runaway slave, Onesimus, a second chance. Today we read this and often come to a very quick judgment and find ourselves taking the side of Onesimus, because we figure that as a believer, Philemon should not have owned a slave anyway. We however are looking at a story out of context when we do that. We must look at the story in the context of the day that it was written. The culture of that day was one in which slavery was an accepted part of how society operated. In that culture, it was as if Onesimus had robbed Philemon of an economic asset. In fact, according to verse 18, Onesimus might have robbed Philemon of money in addition to running away. Philemon needed to forgive Onesimus of his wrong, but he also had to be willing to be patient with him as Onesimus regained Philemon's trust.

As we look at this story and also at the passage from Ephesians, we find that patience is vital to human relationships in three different ways: 1) it affirms a person's worth; 2) it strengthens our submission to God; and 3) it maintains unity as a group of believers. Let's look at each of these consequences of patience.

Patience and Worth

First, we need to understand when we show patience to others we are showing them their worth to us. When we are patient, we show them they are worth our time and the effort it takes to be patient with them. We are not giving up on them because they have wronged us or because they haven't done things our way. This is the same motivation Paul used to ask Philemon to be patient with Onesimus. In verse 16, Paul wrote, "This is especially so to me, but even more to you, both in the flesh and in the Lord." ❺ Paul was telling Philemon that by investing patience in this slave, he would acquire something more valuable—a Christian brother. "For perhaps this is why he was separated from you for a brief time, so that you might get him back permanently, no longer as a slave, but more than a slave—as a dearly loved brother" (vv. 15-16a).

❺ What was the "something more" Paul said Onesimus could be if Philemon would be patient with him?

Paul was taking the opportunity to have Philemon look beyond the culture of that day. A slave was measured in the currency of the day, while we cannot put a price on a Christian brother or sister. Paul knew that and was sharing this with Philemon. ❻ It was Christian brothers like Luke, Timothy, and Mark (2 Tim. 4:11; Philem. 24) who stuck by Paul even when he was imprisoned. Paul knew that he could not put

❻ What three Christian brothers were with Paul in his hour of need?

a value on those men and their patience with him. He knew that he had invested his time, effort, and patience in them earlier and they had repaid him with their presence in his time of need. As modern-day Christians we might see this as contrary to what we studied in the previous lesson—loving others unconditionally, but it is not. Paul knew that the Christian life could not be based on a potential payback. Paul claimed that Onesimus might be "useful" to Philemon, but more than as a slave. Paul knew that Philemon could have someone in his life who would care genuinely for him. We know today as well as Paul knew when he wrote this, there is nothing worth more than a brother or sister who is there for us when we are in need.

Patience and Submission

Second, patience with people is also a part of our submission to God. Paul appealed to Philemon by writing, "although I have great boldness in Christ to command you to do what is right, I appeal, instead, on the basis of love" (vv. 8-9a). Paul was reminding Philemon that as a church leader, Paul had the authority to tell Philemon what he must do. However Paul didn't want to do that; instead he appealed to Philemon on the basis of love. Paul did mention this authority to remind Philemon that he had an obligation to submit to his authority in Christ. ❼ In fact, there is a strong correlation between patience and submission. Impatience implies, "People need to do things on my timetable and my way." When we realize we aren't the one to set the standards and the timetable, then we begin to understand there is someone greater than ourselves who does—to whom we need to submit. God is the One who judges. God is the One who decides how things should be done, and God is the One who sets the timetable when things are to be done. We must learn to submit to Him and His will of how things are to be done and when they are to happen.

❼ What correlation is there between patience and submission?

Patience and Unity

Finally, patience is an important part of maintaining unity in a group. Think about when you are with your friends getting ready to go somewhere, and someone is taking a few extra minutes to get ready. How you react to that person actually begins to set the tone for the day. If you criticize the person for taking too much time they will either hurry or feel rushed, they could argue and cause friction in the group, or they could simply tell everyone to go on, leaving them behind. When you show patience with that person however, they have a tendency to hurry themselves up out of respect for the whole group. Showing patience can lead to greater unity. When someone regularly takes advantage of the patience of others and continually is late or makes the group late, others begin to become frustrated with them and withdraw their offer of patience. So patience must be both offered and received with respect. Paul wanted Philemon to know that he and Onesimus were part of the same team. They might have been slave and master, but now they were brothers in Christ.

❽ Which one of his own writings could Paul have quoted to describe the new unity as Christians between Philemon and Onesimus?

❽ Paul could easily have quoted to Philemon his own writing to the Galatians (3:28), "There is no Jew or Greek, slave or free, male or female; for you are all one in Christ Jesus." Patience both recognizes and maintains this oneness in Christ. Patience helps us see each other as equals, and helps us keep the unity of the Spirit (Eph. 4:3).

Today, we have to learn to look at others with patience because the patience we show them can help them understand Christ's love more deeply. When we interact with other Christian brothers and sisters with patience, we begin to develop a contagious Christian community that takes the message of Christ through patience to those outside the group.

SMALL-GROUP TIME: **After presenting the teaching material, ask students to divide back into small groups and discuss the "Do What?" questions. Small-group facilitators should lead the discussions and set the model for being open and honest in responding to questions.**

Do What? (15 minutes)

Making It Personal

1. Why do you think Paul mentioned the fact that he was now elderly and a prisoner? What role did this play in his appeal on behalf of Onesimus?

2. What do you think Paul, deep down, really wanted Philemon to do in relation to Onesimus?
   - ☐ Let Onesimus stay with Paul to care for him.
   - ☐ Let Onesimus go.
   - ☐ Give Onesimus another chance as a slave.
   - ☐ Keep Onesimus as a slave, but treat him more like a family member.
   - ☐ Other ______________________________

3. How do you see yourself like Onesimus now:
   - ☐ I need someone to give me another chance.
   - ☐ I need someone to talk to someone else on my behalf.
   - ☐ I need to feel more like a brother or sister and less like a slave.
   - ☐ I need to feel useful to someone else.
   - ☐ I need someone to be patient with me so I can prove myself.
   - ☐ I feel like Philemon—I need to learn how to give people a little slack.
   - ☐ Other ______________

Small-group facilitators should reinforce the "LifePoint" for this session, making sure that students' questions are invited and addressed honestly.

LifePoint Review

Patience develops with time and cannot be rushed.

"Do" Points

These "Do" Points will help you begin to experience this week's "LifePoint." Be open and honest as you discuss the action points within your small group.

1. Write a definition of "patience." Read your definition for the group and as a group come up with a "group" definition of patience. How can you be more patient according to your definition? As a group, come up with a plan of action for the week.

2. Perform an assessment of the role that the patience of others has played in your life. When did someone show patience with you and how did it affect your life? When could someone have shown you patience, and they chose not to? Whom do you know right now whom you could encourage as he or she goes through a stressful time? Who could use more patience from you right now?

3. Be an advocate for patience this week in the life of someone else. Find someone to offer patience to this week. Avoid the chance to stand on a religious soapbox regarding patience, but encourage your friends to offer patience to others this week. Encourage your friends to offer someone a "second chance." Instead of giving up on someone you know who is struggling, pray for him or her. Imagine that patience is something that is contagious and will spread to others by your actions.

Encourage students to list prayer needs for others in their books so they can pray for one another during the week.

Assign a student coordinator in each small group to gather the group's requests and e-mail them to the group members.

Prayer Connection:

This is the time to encourage, support, and pray for each other in our journeys to trust God and seek out real and personal encounters with Him.

Share prayer needs and requests with the group, especially those related to hearing from and responding to God. Your group facilitator will close your time in prayer.

Prayer Needs:

Encourage students to dig a little deeper by completing a "Now What?" assignment before the next time you meet.

Remind students about the "Get Ready" short daily Bible readings and related questions at the beginning of session 5.

Now What?

Remind them again this week that they are loved!

Deepen your understanding of who God is and His desire for us to have an authentic Christian community, and continue the journey you've begun today by choosing one of the following assignments to complete this week:

Option #1:

If you enjoy writing, take time this week to keep a journal about the times when you either give someone patience or experience patience. Journal about times when you feel like your patience is being tested and times when you wish others would offer you more patience. Find a person you know who needs patience. This week find a way to offer him or her patience. Note how you feel and how you perceive him or her to feel by your actions.

Option #2:

Take some time this week and rewrite the message of Philemon in your own words. The important thing is to grasp and communicate the meaning of the passage. Make it a personal letter to yourself. Be prepared to share your thoughts next week with your small group.

Bible Reference Notes

Use these notes to gain further understanding of the text as you study on your own.

Ephesians 4:1

I . . . urge you. Stylistically, Paul moves from the indicative ("This is the way things are") to the imperative ("This is what must be done").
walk worthy of the calling. We don't do what God wants in order for Him to call us to Him, but to be worthy of the grace He has already shown in calling us.

Ephesians 4:2

humility. Humility isn't putting ourselves down, but rather seeing ourselves in the context of the fact that all of God's children are equally valuable, and we are all subject to Him. Humility is the key to the growth of healthy relationships between people.
gentleness. Gentleness is the quality of strength under control, like a thoroughbred horse.
patience. A vital aspect of love (1 Cor. 13:4), patience is giving people the time they need to evolve and grow.
accepting one another in love. The New International Version translates this as "bearing with one another." This is really another aspect of patience—a tolerance of the other person's faults.

Philemon 9

on the basis of love. Christian love, not a grudging obedience to Paul's command, was the only basis on which a true brotherly relationship could be built between Philemon and Onesimus.
an elderly man . . . prisoner. While not appealing to his apostolic authority, Paul certainly appeals to the respect Philemon has for him. Paul's stress on his imprisonment (vv. 1,9,23) may be to hint that he too knows the limitations of a form of enslavement.

Philemon 11

useless . . . useful. There is a play on words here. These two words, which sound very similar in Greek, share a root word that was pronounced the same way as the word for Christ (*christos* means *Christ; chestos* means *useful*). Through Christ, Onesimus (whose name also means *useful*), formerly a useless, disobedient slave, has now become truly useful as a brother in the Lord.

Philemon 12

In spite of his love, Paul had to send Onesimus back, since harboring a runaway slave was a serious crime. The reality of his conversion would be seen in his willingness to return to Philemon and face up to the consequences of what he had done. Christian slaves were expected to view their work for their master as work done for the Lord (Col. 3:22-25).

Philemon 16

in the flesh and in the Lord. "In the flesh" Onesimus is just a slave, but "in the Lord" he is now Philemon's spiritual brother.

Notes

Session

5

SHARING ONE ANOTHER'S BURDENS

Connections Prep

MAIN "LIFEPOINT": As Christians we need others in our lives.

To reinforce the "LifePoint," leaders and small-group facilitators should understand the following more detailed CheckPoints and "Do" Points.

5

BIBLE STUDY CHECKPOINTS:

- Understand why Scripture calls us to share our lives with others instead of being independent.
- Consider the various ways we are called to bear one another's burdens.
- Understand the difference between sharing one another's burdens and encouraging codependency.

LIFE CHANGE "DO" POINTS:

- Give at least one hour of assistance this week to someone who could benefit from a skill you possess.
- Recognize one burden you have in your life that you have chosen to struggle with alone, and share it with a trusted Christian friend.
- Reach out to people who may need a listening ear.

PREPARATION:

- ☐ Review the leader book for this session and prepare your teaching in advance.
- ☐ Determine how you will divide students into small discussion groups.
- ☐ Recruit mature students or adults as small-group facilitators. Be sure these facilitators plan to attend your meeting.

REQUIRED SUPPLIES:

- ☐ *Contagious Community: Living Beyond Yourself* leader book for each group facilitator
- ☐ *Contagious Community: Living Beyond Yourself* student book for each student
- ☐ Pen or pencil for each student

"Get Ready" is primarily for students, but leaders and facilitators will benefit from these devotionals as well.

Get Ready

Read one of these short Bible passages each day, and spend a few minutes of focused time with God. Be sure to jot down any insights you receive.

MONDAY

Read Galatians 6:2.

Are you more eager to help others with their burdens or get help for yours? What can you do today to help someone who has a burden?

TUESDAY

Read Galatians 6:5.

What "load" is the heaviest for you to carry right now? Is this load a necessity in your life? How could you make this load lighter today?

WEDNESDAY

Read Ecclesiastes 4:9.

What are some things in your life that you are doing by yourself right now? How many of those things can you ask for help with? What keeps you from asking for help for those things?

THURSDAY

Read Ecclesiastes 4:10.

How do you react to others when they fall? Do you rush to their aid to help them up? Do you find yourself standing to the side laughing at them? Do you look for ways to take advantage of them while they are down?

FRIDAY

Read Ecclesiastes 4:11.

Is the world warm or cold to you? How could you benefit from having someone in your life to share your experiences with?

SATURDAY

Read Ecclesiastes 4:12a.

What is something that is trying to overpower you right now? Do you have trouble trying to resist a certain temptation? Where can you turn for help when something is about to overtake you?

SUNDAY

Read Ecclesiastes 4:12b.

Who are your friends? Would you say that your friends are a part of your cord? Is God a part of your cord?

LARGE-GROUP OPENING: Get everyone's attention. Make announcements. Open your session with a prayer. Read the "LifePoint" to the students.

5

LifePoint

As Christians we need others in our lives.

SMALL-GROUP TIME: Instruct students to separate into groups of four to eight, preferably in a circle configuration. Call on the mature student or adult leaders you recruited to facilitate each small group through this "Say What?" segment.

Say What? (15 minutes)

Random Question of the Week:

Would you rather have a pound of quarters or a pound of gourmet coffee? Why?

Group Experience: Describe Your Falls

Share the following questions with the students in your small group and allow each student to answer. Encourage students to share their answers to the questions. The purpose of this experience is to allow students to share their thoughts with the group and also begin thinking about the groups with whom they spend their time.

LARGE-GROUP TIME: Direct students to turn to face the front for this teaching time. Be sure you can make eye contact with each student in the room. Encourage them to follow along and take notes in their student books.

Share the "So What?" information with students. You may modify it to meet your needs. Be sure to highlight the underlined information, which gives answers to the student book questions and fill-in-the-blanks (shown in the margins).

1. How do you describe your attitude when it comes to falling?
   - ☐ I'm a klutz; I fall all the time.
   - ☐ I'm like a cat—I always fall on my feet.
   - ☐ I don't climb too high, that way, I don't have too far to fall.
   - ☐ I've fallen a lot, but only because I've climbed a lot and taken a lot of risks.
   - ☐ I would have never learned to walk if it wasn't for falling.
   - ☐ I should probably wear a helmet and pads—just in case.
   - ☐ I'm made of rubber; I bounce back up after each fall.
   - ☐ Other ______________

2. What scars on your body do you have from falling? Are there any we can see? How did you get them? Do they serve as a reminder for you about how you got them?

3. What is the hardest fall you have ever taken physically? emotionally? socially? spiritually?

So What? (30 minutes)

Teaching Outline

I. We Need Other People
God designed us this way

II. Learning from the Bible
A. Galatians 6:2
B. Ecclesiastes 4:9-12

III. Bearing One Another's Burdens

IV. Sharing the Burden of Work
Working as a team

V. Sharing the Burden of Failure
Everyone experiences failures

VI. Sharing the Burden of Protection

We Need Other People

Today's culture is teaching teenagers the need for independence. We hear it everywhere we go. Instead of going to a movie, students can download one to their computer, watch it on a personal DVD player, or on their iPod. The culture today is teaching teens to be like the hero in the old western movies, be independent and ride off into the sunset alone on his horse. This went on to say, "I don't need anyone, just me and my horse." While this rugged individualism can be entertaining and enticing in the movies, we must learn that it doesn't make for a very full life.

❶ What Old Testament Scripture tells us that God designed us to need other people?

❷ What are four reasons why we need other people?

We were created to need other people—not because of some gaping weakness in our lives, but because God designed us this way. Scripture confirms this. ❶ Genesis 2:18 states, "It is not good for the man to be alone." Here it is significant that no animal was able to complete Adam; it had to be a human companion.

5

❷ We need other people for many reasons; we need someone we can relate to, meaning, we need communication among our peers. We also have the need to share our experiences and joy; we need to communicate thoughts, ideas, and feelings to someone else rather than keep them to ourselves. Last, but not least, we need someone with whom we can share the burdens of our life. We do not live in a perfect world. On the contrary, life can be hard. As part of the curse on Adam and Eve when they left the Garden of Eden, God told them, "The ground is cursed because of you. You will eat from it by means of painful labor all the days of your life" (Gen. 3:17). Unfortunately the labor of agriculture isn't the only difficult part of life. We also have to learn to deal with the emotional aspects of life. We must learn to deal with failure, peer pressure, and family issues. These are more manageable in our lives when we don't try to be the hero and bolt head-first through them, but rather as we become part of a supportive Christian community.

Before the session, enlist a youth to read Galatians 6:2 and Ecclesiastes 4:9-12.

Learning from the Bible

2 Carry one another's burdens; in this way you will fulfill the law of Christ.

9 Two are better than one because they have a good reward for their efforts: 10 For if either falls, his companion can lift him up; but pity the one who falls without another to lift him up; 11 Also, if two lie down together, they can keep warm; but how can one person alone keep warm? 12 And if somebody overpowers one person, two can resist him. A cord of three strands is not easily broken.

Bearing One Another's Burdens

How important are friends to you? What are the benefits of having friends in your life? Hopefully as you read these verses you are reminded of the importance of having true, godly friends in your life. Not simple acquaintances, but friends with whom you can share your life.

The movie *Seabiscuit* is about a horse that had been written off by many people. This horse however had people who believed in his potential, and he came back to become one of horse racing's most famous legends. The key to the horse's success is that three men were willing to go against the belief of most people and believe in the horse's potential. He was bought by an owner who was trying to put his life back together after a tragedy; he was cared for by a trainer who many thought was a little crazy and washed up; he was ridden by a jockey whose life had disintegrated due to failure, abuse, and drinking. What a dream team for this horse! Nevertheless, they were able to forge a bond and became a place where each of them were encouraged and lifted up after they stumbled. Together they were not easily broken, just like we must be today as a Christian community.

We must see each other as on the same team. We cannot focus on the failures and faults of each other, but we must look at the potential and the good that each of us is capable of with Christ living in us. We must learn to look at each other and be willing to help share the burdens of each other. This can be done in three different areas of life—work, failure, and protection.

Sharing the Burden of Work

❸ How can you build and develop the Christian community while performing work projects together?

Christian communities can share the burden of work. Ecclesiastes 4:9 states that two are better than one "because they have a good reward for their efforts." Think about it; if you have a job to do, do you not benefit from having someone help you? Would it be faster for you to rake a yard full of leaves by yourself or with a friend to help you? Obviously, it would be faster with a helpful friend. As a Christian community how quickly could you take a team of teenagers to an elderly person's house and rake their leaves? Would it be quicker to do it as an individual or as a group? The group is always faster! When you decide to work together toward the same goal, the time the task takes is cut dramatically. ❸ Working together as a group creates a bond that comes from mutual dependence. Everyone has a portion of the task and we must learn to trust that they are fulfilling their portion of the project. It also provides an opportunity to talk in an informal way with the pressure off. Some people can share their thoughts and concerns more openly when there is no pressure to share and the focus is on the task at hand. While the purpose of sharing the burden of work is not to get someone to talk, realizing the opportunity is there helps us become more sensitive to the hurts and needs of others.

Sharing the burden of work also helps us learn to work together as a team. Think about the movie, *Shrek*. In the movie, Shrek and Donkey have the task before them of saving the princess. In order to save the princess, Shrek must learn to work with Donkey—something he is not used to. Shrek must learn to allow someone else to help him, and the benefit of trusting Donkey to help allows Shrek to reach his goal—saving the Princess. We must be like this, learning to share the burdens we have before us with others. The Christian life doesn't require us to live without others. If we do not learn to trust others in the work at hand, we do not benefit from the Christian community that the work creates.

Sharing the Burden of Failure

Second, people form a bond together in sharing the burden of failure. Ecclesiastes 4:10 states that if two people are truly living life together, "if either falls, his companion can lift him up; but pity the one who falls without another to lift him up." Think about this analogy, if you fall down, having someone beside you to offer you a hand and pick you up takes all of the effort off yourself. You don't have to get up on your own! You must however trust the person offering you assistance in order to benefit from it.

One of the hardest realities of life is that we all sometimes fail. The great baseball player, Babe Ruth, was a home run king. He also struck out more times than he had home runs. The great President, Abraham Lincoln, lost more elections than he won. We even like to celebrate and laugh at other people's failures. That's why so many tabloid magazines are available—to show us the faults of others. We watch video "bloopers" on television and the Internet because we like to see what happens to others and that often makes us feel better by realizing that others fail.

❹ What are three reasons why failure can be more difficult to handle when you live life by yourself—keeping others at a distance?

The reality of failure is always there. The question is not will you fail, but what will happen when you do? ❹ <u>If you live your life by yourself—keeping others at a distance—failure becomes more difficult to handle. When you get down on yourself, there is no one there to encourage you and help you believe in yourself again. There is no one to remind you of your accomplishments and no one to get others to believe in you.</u>

Some people look at church as a place where only the spiritually successful are welcome. Many look at church as the place where the smiling and happy get together to talk about how much God loves them and about how great things are in their lives. It's a place for only happy families to come, smile, sit together, and talk with other happy families. While it's true that we should have a smile on our hearts as we rejoice over the blessings God has given to each of us, that is only a portion of the story. Church is also a place where we can be encouraged after we strike out or make a mistake in our lives. The church is supposed to be a place where we develop friendships that look past our successes and help us through our failures. Jesus chose those initial 12 disciples from ordinary men. None of them were extraordinary in the eyes of the religious leaders, if anything they were labeled as "sinners and tax collectors." For the church to embrace anything less than welcoming people regardless of their failures begins to create an atmosphere of false representation. We encourage people to wear masks instead of be who they really are. A truly redemptive Christian community is a community in which all falseness is discarded, and in which we let each other see us as we are.

Sharing the Burden of Protection

Finally, we must realize that once we leave the redemptive Christian community and go back into the world, we are going into a hard, tough, and difficult place. The outside world doesn't rejoice with us when we rejoice, nor do they cry when we cry. The outside world is hungry for true community where they can feel loved and protected. For years police and law-enforcement organizations have claimed that many teenagers join gangs because they are looking for a place of acceptance, and if being accepted means doing something illegal or questionable, the desire for acceptance wins many times. People desire to be a part of a community that offers them protection—one that is constantly watching each others' back.

❺ What are two kinds of threats we might need to help each other withstand?

Ecclesiastes 4:11-12 states, "Also, if two lie down together, they can keep warm; but how can one person alone keep warm? And if somebody overpowers one person, two can resist him. A cord of three strands is not easily broken." ❺ <u>This passage refers to both protection from natural threats as well as protection from human threats.</u> The cold weather is just as threatening to others today as it was in biblical times. You will notice the cold more severely and quickly alone than when you are with others, because by yourself, no one is there for comfort and warmth.

Of course, we are not saying that the Christian community should literally cuddle up and keep warm! The point is the world can be and is a very cold place where we as Christians will face many dangers. As Christians we do not have to weather the storms of life alone. If we choose to live as a loner, who will be there when we get bad news about a loved one? Who will be there to comfort us when we fail a test (that we truly studied for) and who will be there when we feel alone in the world? Who can help warm our spirits? Who can we count on for practical help—someone to help us study for a subject we really don't understand, someone to talk through the tough times with, or even someone to sit beside us when we visit with a sick loved one? We tend to downplay the importance of friendships that move past the surface level—until we need them, then we wish we would have done more to make sure we had someone to help us "keep warm" when tough times come.

When we are in physical danger, having a friend around is always a benefit. What happens if you walk through a parking lot late one night and find your car missing? Do you find comfort in knowing a friend is there? Do you remember as a child the comfort of having a friend with you when you were scared of the dark? Who is part of your support system "cord" that keeps you feeling safe when it feels like you are in danger?

❻ What is Keith Miller's definition of intimacy, as it relates to sharing our struggles with others?

Because we all suffer from struggles like these, we need to open our lives and let others in. We need someone beside us sometimes just to provide us comfort and help us relax in a situation. ❻ Think about this definition of intimacy from Keith Miller: "the sharing of one's reality in one place where the listeners just listen and share, but don't condemn, shame or try to fix the one sharing." Such sharing does not require us to be able to answer all of life's questions. It just means that we are willing to listen to others and care for them—we don't have to have all of the answers. Learning to share each other's burdens is not a test we must cram for, rather, it is a lifestyle that understands the importance and need for others in our lives.

SMALL-GROUP TIME: After presenting the teaching material, ask students to divide back into small groups and discuss the "Do What?" questions. Small-group facilitators should lead the discussions and set the model for being open and honest in responding to questions.

Do What? (15 minutes)

Making It Personal

1. What is your biggest burden right now? Do you feel like you are about to be overpowered by that burden? Why?

2. What kind of help and support do you need most right now?
   - ☐ Someone willing to share the burdens at work or with chores at home (v. 9)
   - ☐ Someone willing to help "pull me up" after I've fallen down (v. 10)
   - ☐ Someone willing to stand with me in the face of natural dangers like sickness and disease (v. 11)
   - ☐ Someone willing to stand with me when others try to threaten me or others (v. 12)
   - ☐ other ______________

3. What do you need to do to develop a "cord of three stands" that will keep you from being broken in times of stress?
   - ☐ I need to be more supportive of others so they will be there to support me.
   - ☐ I need to be more open and honest about my needs, so people will know how to really help me.
   - ☐ I need to be more a part of what my group is doing.
   - ☐ I need to include God in my "cord."

- ☐ I need to stop trying to figure things out on my own and trust God with my problems.
- ☐ Other ______________________________

Small-group facilitators should reinforce the "LifePoint" for this session, making sure that students' questions are invited and addressed honestly.

LifePoint Review

As Christians we need others in our lives.

"Do" Points

These "Do" Points will help you begin to experience this week's "LifePoint." Be open and honest as you discuss the action points within your small group.

1. Give at least one hour of assistance this week to someone who could benefit from a skill you possess. Are you good at technological things? Could you sit down with a peer or adult who isn't and take the time to show them some tips about the computer? Are you doing well in school? Could you spend some time tutoring a classmate? Do you like to cook? Could you take the time to cook for a single-mom family one night so she has time to spend with her kids? Find a way to use the gifts that God has given you to help others.

2. Recognize one burden you have in your life that you have chosen to struggle with alone and share it with a trusted Christian friend. It's time to find someone that you trust (someone who has shown in the past that he or she can be relied upon to keep things confidential) to share your burden with. It is also important to find someone who is a Christian (one who shares the commitment to "carry one another's burdens" in order to fulfill what Christ has called us to do and be). By finding someone to share your burden with, you are finding someone to walk beside you in the hard times. You might want to talk to an adult you trust or even look within this group to find someone to whom God might be leading you. If you are unsure of who you need to talk to, begin with a youth worker or pastor.

3. Reach out to people who may need a listening ear. When you look around the cafeteria, do you see people sitting alone? Can you think of someone who always seems to be on the outside of the bigger group? Pay attention when people talk and you'll begin to notice who is going through a tough time. Maybe someone shares a prayer request during this group time or maybe you hear of someone's need. Take the time this week to listen. Follow up with a phone call later this week to get updates. This helps keep you informed and reminds them that your interest in sharing their burden was more than momentary.

Encourage students to list prayer needs for others in their books so they can pray for one another during the week.

Assign a student coordinator in each small group to gather the group's requests and e-mail them to the group members.

Prayer Connection:

This is the time to encourage, support, and pray for each other in our journeys to trust God and seek out real and personal encounters with Him.

Share prayer needs and requests with the group, especially those related to hearing from and responding to God. Your group facilitator will close your time in prayer.

Prayer Needs:

Encourage students to dig a little deeper by completing a "Now What?" assignment before the next time you meet.

Remind students about the "Get Ready" short daily Bible readings and related questions at the beginning of session 6.

Now What?

Remind them again this week that they are loved!

Deepen your understanding of who God is and His desire for us to have an authentic Christian community, and continue the journey you've begun today by choosing one of the following assignments to complete this week:

Option #1:

If you enjoy writing, take the time this week to keep a journal about the week and note the burdens you experience. Take care to note who helps you with those burdens, if anyone does. Note how you feel when you go through the burdens with a friend and how you feel when you are left to carry your burdens alone. Is there anything you are holding on to this week that you could share with someone else but haven't done so yet? What is keeping you from doing that?

Option #2:

Take some time this week and rewrite Ecclesiastes 4:9-12 in your own words. Feel free to paraphrase the passage or rewrite it in a paragraph form. The important thing is to grasp and communicate the meaning of the passage. Be prepared to share your thoughts next week with your small group.

Bible Reference Notes

Use these notes to gain further understanding of the text as you study on your own:

Galatians 6:2

Carry one another's burdens. Mutual burden-bearing lies at the heart of Christian fellowship.
burdens. A heavy, crushing weight that a single individual cannot carry. The Greek word used here is different than the word used for "load" (in some versions also translated as "burden") in verse 5. The word used in verse 5 is used to describe the small, individual pack a hiker or soldier carries. It is also the same word used by Jesus in Matthew 11:30 to describe the burden (load) of His yoke, signifying that each of us has a burden (load) to carry.
law of Christ. The law of love (5:14), which stands in sharp contrast to Old Testament law.

Ecclesiastes 4:9-12

The human solution to life's misery is companionship. This oft-quoted passage is not entirely positive. Life is better with a companion, but one still experiences work, falls, cold, and attacks from outsiders. Even with intimate friendship, we still live under the sun, subject to all the troubles life brings.

Session 6

WORKING WITH EACH OTHER

Connections Prep

MAIN "LIFEPOINT": Working together helps Christians grow.

To reinforce the "LifePoint," leaders and small-group facilitators should understand the following more detailed CheckPoints and "Do" Points.

BIBLE STUDY CHECKPOINTS:

- Recognize the benefits of working together as Christians.
- Find the advantage of learning to work with a wide variety of people.
- Consider how working together as a team means encouraging and watching out for one another.

LIFE CHANGE "DO" POINTS:

- Participate in one project or mission your church is involved in.
- Recognize the work someone else is doing, and give them encouragement for their hard work.
- Find a way to "protect" someone in your church who works diligently at a position that makes them susceptible to the scrutiny of others.

PREPARATION:

- ☐ Review the leader book for this session and prepare your teaching in advance.
- ☐ Determine how you will divide students into small discussion groups.
- ☐ Recruit mature students or adults as small-group facilitators. Be sure these facilitators plan to attend your meeting.

REQUIRED SUPPLIES:

- ☐ *Contagious Community: Living Beyond Yourself* leader book for each group facilitator
- ☐ *Contagious Community: Living Beyond Yourself* student book for each student
- ☐ Pen or pencil for each student

"Get Ready" is primarily for students, but leaders and facilitators will benefit from these devotionals as well.

Get Ready

Read one of these short Bible passages each day, and spend a few minutes of focused time with God. Be sure to jot down any insights you receive.

MONDAY

Read 1 Corinthians 3:9.

How are you a partner with God in His work? How are you doing in your partnership with Him? How would you rate your performance on the job? How are you God's "field" or His "building"? How well do you think you are partnering with God?

TUESDAY

Read Acts 18:1-3.

Have you ever been forced to do something you didn't want to do? How did you feel when that happened? When have you done something you didn't want to do and found that God used your experience for something good? Why did Paul stay with Priscilla and Aquila?

WEDNESDAY

Read Acts 18:4.

How do you feel when you have the opportunity to share your faith with someone who is skeptical? Have you ever taken advantage of one of these opportunities? Have you ever purposefully avoided an opportunity to share your faith? What would help you have more confidence when you have these opportunities?

THURSDAY

Read Acts 18:5-6.

Have you ever experienced rejection? When you fail, how good are you at shaking it off and moving on? How do you handle rejection?

FRIDAY

Read Acts 18:7-8.

Have you ever had the opportunity to share your faith with someone and see them come to faith in Christ? If not, what could you do to change that? Are you making the most of the opportunities you have?

SATURDAY

Read Acts 18:9.
What causes you to keep silent when you know you should be speaking up? Have you ever spoken up for something you believe in, regardless of how others might view your opinion? What do you believe so strongly in that you would stand up and speak out in favor of it?

SUNDAY

Read Acts 18:10-11.
Do you have people in your life who are your support? How do you recognize these people? Is it possible that God has put these people in your life and you have yet to recognize them?

LARGE-GROUP OPENING:
Get everyone's attention. Make announcements. Open your session with a prayer. Read the "LifePoint" to students.

LifePoint

Working together helps Christians grow.

SMALL-GROUP TIME:
Instruct students to separate into groups of four to eight, preferably in a circle configuration.

Call on the mature student or adult leaders you recruited to facilitate each small group through this "Say What?" segment.

Say What? (15 minutes)

Random Question of the Week:
If all the cars in the world stopped working, how would you travel from your house to school?

Group Experience: Matching Sidekicks
Share the following questions with the students in your small group and allow each student to answer. Encourage students to share their answers to the questions. The purpose of this experience is to allow students to share their thoughts with the group and also begin thinking about the groups with whom they spend their time.

1. With which famous sidekick would you like to spend time?
   - ☐ Patrick (Spongebob Squarepants)
   - ☐ Robin (Batman)
   - ☐ Barney Fife (The Andy Griffith Show)
   - ☐ I'm like Mr. Incredible—I work alone!
   - ☐ Goofy (Mickey Mouse)
   - ☐ Vinnie (Paul Jr.—Orange County choppers)
   - ☐ I thought sidekick was a Chuck Norris movie.
   - ☐ I thought a sidekick was a phone.
   - ☐ Other ______________________________

2. Who is your "sidekick"? What do you do with your sidekick? How much do you trust this person?

3. If you were going to pick the perfect sidekick, what qualities or characteristics would you expect him or her to have?

LARGE-GROUP TIME: **Direct students to turn to face the front for this teaching time. Be sure you can make eye contact with each student in the room. Encourage them to follow along and take notes in their student books.**

Share the "So What?" information with students. You may modify it to meet your needs. Be sure to highlight the underlined information, which gives answers to the student book questions and fill-in-the-blanks (shown in the margins).

So What? (30 minutes)

Teaching Outline

I. Working Alongside of God

A. God uses all kinds of people

B. Work with others

C. Find a way to contribute

II. Learning from the Bible

A. 1 Corinthians 3:9

B. Acts 18:1-11

III. The Camaraderie of Working Together

A. Create a bond

B. Work for something bigger than yourself

IV. Building a Team

Allow all team members to use their talents

V. Watching Each Other's Back

Working Alongside of God

Society today stresses the importance of getting a good job. Newspapers have a "Help Wanted" section that helps people find a paying job. Why do people work? Is the necessity of money the only reason? It shouldn't be. People also have a need to connect with others in a place where they can use the skills God has given them. As teenagers, you might not have the ability to get a paying job at a restaurant, grocery store, or at the nearest mall, but you still have the same needs to connect with others and use your talents. Your Christian community is a place where you can use your talents and skills as you learn to work with others as a team. Think about 1 Corinthians 3:9—you could even work alongside God as you help share the gospel message inside your church. You could help teach children, assist with various teams within the church, help maintain the church's landscaping (or even plant some flowers where there are none). Regardless of what you do, you must understand you are not only working with others, you are also working alongside God to accomplish His purposes.

❶ What three qualities are often required to work well together with others?

❷ What are three reasons why working together well is important to being a contagious community?

Even as you work with God, you must realize He uses all kinds of people. This might sound like it takes some of the glamour away. ❶ People are not always easy to work with. Working with people requires qualities we would expect—patience, love, and forgiveness. However, working well together is important for developing a contagious community. ❷ Three reasons we need to learn to work well with each other: (1) People want to be a part of a community where their contribution is needed. We all need to be needed. (2) Working together well means things are done efficiently and goals are reached. We need to be a part of something bigger than just "hanging out" with our friends. We might enjoy it at first but eventually we would recognize the work at hand is not getting done without working together. (3) Working together well builds relationships. People learn they can trust and rely on each other. When we learn to appreciate each other's unique gifts and contributions to the task at hand, we begin to value each member of the team.

As teenagers we tend to shy away from others who are not like us. We aren't prejudice against them but they often intimidate us. Many times we are happy to let others do the work that needs to be done because we are still young.

❸ Give five examples of the variety of people with whom Paul worked.

Paul was successful in his missionary works due in great part to his ability to work well with a wide variety of people. ❸ In Acts 18, we find Paul working with a Jewish couple from Rome (Priscilla and Aquila), a Roman citizen who had been a leader in the Jerusalem church (Silas), a young man from southern Asia Minor (Timothy), a convert to Judaism (Titus Justus), and a Greek synagogue official (Crispus). By looking at this story in Acts, perhaps we can learn some things about how we can do a better job of working together with others.

The movie *Dumb and Dumber* is typical of many teenagers' views of work. After going out to look for work (after being fired from his job as a limo driver), Lloyd Christmas comes back from a day of job hunting and proclaims no jobs are to be found, "unless you want to work 40 hours a week." Many of us are like that. We view work as something that needs to happen by someone—anyone—other than us. We don't like to work when it doesn't pertain to something we're deeply interested in. On the other hand, many of us don't mind working when we are doing something we are passionate about, and when our skills are used, and we feel like we are contributing to something. It is important that we, in the Christian community, help believers find a way to contribute and use their skills for the work of the Lord.

In the church of Paul's day, they had more than one "Lloyd Christmas." Paul wrote about these people in 2 Thessalonians 3:10, "If anyone isn't willing to work, he should not eat." However, Paul was able to put together a strong team of people who worked together well and shared in the success of Paul's missionary journeys. Our focal passage from Acts is a good example of some of the people with whom he worked. This passage also helps us to see some key elements of working together.

Before the session, enlist a youth to read 1 Corinthians 3:9 and Acts 18:1-11.

Learning from the Bible

9 For we are God's co-workers. You are God's field, God's building.

1 After this, he left from Athens and went to Corinth, 2 where he found a Jewish man named Aquila, a native of Pontus, who had recently come from Italy with his wife Priscilla because Claudius had ordered all the Jews to leave Rome. Paul came to them, 3 and being of the same occupation, stayed with them and worked, for they were tentmakers by trade. 4 He reasoned in the synagogue every Sabbath and tried to persuade both Jews and Greeks.

5 When Silas and Timothy came down from Macedonia, Paul was occupied with preaching the message and solemnly testified to the Jews that the Messiah is Jesus. 6 But when they resisted and blasphemed, he shook out his clothes and told them, "Your blood is on your own heads! I am clean. From now on I will go to the Gentiles." 7 So he left there and went to the house of a man named Titius Justus, a worshiper of God,

whose house was next door to the synagogue. [8] Crispus, the leader of the synagogue, believed the Lord, along with his whole household; and many of the Corinthians, when they heard, believed and were baptized.

[9] Then the Lord said to Paul in a night vision, "Don't be afraid, but keep on speaking and don't be silent. [10] For I am with you, and no one will lay a hand on you to hurt you, because I have many people in this city." [11] And he stayed there a year and six months, teaching the word of God among them.

How important are friends to you? What are the benefits of having friends in your life?

The Camaraderie of Working Together

As we discussed in our last session, working together helps bring groups together. We can connect with another person by sharing a project or mission with him or her. Working together in this way creates a bond that comes from a common dependence on each other.

❹ With whom did Paul share his profession of tentmaking?

❹ The Apostle Paul had a special reason for such camaraderie with Priscilla and Aquila since they were all tentmakers. Today, we might read about this and be surprised. We might say, "I thought Paul was a missionary!" He was. However, in those times, people were not always paid to be missionaries or preachers. Paul said it was right that they be paid (1 Cor. 9:13-14), but still it didn't happen for him. Paul even showed some hesitancy about asking for pay for himself (1 Cor. 9:15-18). Since Paul wasn't concerned about getting paid for his missionary journeys, he often supported himself by his tentmaking.

6

❺ Why was it appropriate that Paul was a tentmaker?

❺ It was very appropriate that Paul was a tentmaker since tents are the homes of travelers and Paul was not someone who stayed in one place for long. Perhaps Paul had traveling in common with Priscilla and Aquila. They started out in Pontus, went to Rome, but then they had been told to leave Rome by a decree of Claudius. They were travelers like Paul, and their paths crossed in Corinth. They made their tents of goat-hair cloth, which was a notable export of Paul's native province of Cicilia and was called *Cicilium* after the region. The cloth is rough, tough, and was the fabric of choice for tents because it was designed to withstand the weather. Such a tough cloth took hard work and skill. Paul and this couple spent time together trading secrets and learning from each other as they worked.

Paul, Priscilla, and Aquila experienced camaraderie because they chose to work together for something bigger than them—Christ. Priscilla and Aquila were respected teachers who later even corrected Apollos, himself a respected leader (Acts 18:24-26). Strong leaders sometimes clash, and personalities sometimes pull people apart, but there is no evidence this happened between Paul, Priscilla, and Aquila. They experienced camaraderie by working together as members of a team.

Building a Team

Championship sports teams don't just show up for the championship game. They have worked together in previous practices, scrimmages, and games to prepare for the championship. They realize that everyone has a role to play, and everyone is allowed to use their talents to help the team succeed. If the center of the football team decided the night before the championship that he wanted to be the receiver, he would cause problems—he would be out of position. Great sports teams are great because they learn to depend on each other; they know everyone has a position and a responsibility on the field or court. We need to realize that God has given each of us talents to use with others as a part of a team.

❻ What did Timothy and Silas enable Paul to do when they came to Macedonia?

Paul and his associates were quite a team as well. In Acts 18:5, we are told that when Silas and Timothy came from Macedonia, "Paul was occupied with preaching the message." ❻ The implication of this passage is that Paul was able to focus on preaching and not focus on tentmaking, while Timothy and Silas pitched in and earned or raised money. These men operated like tag-team wrestlers in that when one person got tired, someone else was there to step in for them. Timothy and Silas had been in Berea after Paul was harassed into leaving the area. They were probably able to work in a more low-key way, so as not to draw attention from Jewish leadership. Now they were coming again to join Paul, and they made it possible for him to do what he was supposed to do—preach. They also added to Paul's efforts because they aided Paul in the writing several of his New Testament letters (2 Cor. 1:1; Col. 1:1; 1 Thess. 1:1; 2 Thess. 1:1; Philem. 1).

❼ Who was part of Paul's team who gave his house to be used by Paul and others?

❽ Why was his home's location significant?

❼ Paul had another team member who helped him in his work. Titius Justus was a part of the team we know very little about, except that he offered his home to the disciples for their use. He might not have been skilled in preaching and teaching like Paul, but he offered what was available to him—his home. ❽ His home was extremely important because it was next door to the local synagogue. More Christians were being driven out of the synagogues daily, but Titius Justus' house was available for them to find a place of refuge and to see a familiar face—Crispus—who was a part of the leadership team who had himself been a former synagogue ruler.

❾ What is one instance in Scripture where Paul shared the credit for God's gift of success?

In order to build a strong leadership team, we must realize each person has talents and gifts that are unique to the team as a whole. Paul compares the church to a body in 1 Corinthians 12. He points out that each part of the body has a job to do. Eyes can't hear; ears can't smell; and noses can't see; and likewise we all are gifted to do certain things. This means we must all learn to use our gifts to help out our team, and also, it means no one person gets all of the credit for success. ❾ Paul gave Apollos credit for God's gift of success in his life (1 Cor. 3:6) when he noted, "I planted, Apollos watered, but God gave the growth."

Watching Each Other's Back

Finally, working together as a team means "watching each other's back." Just like the movies when the hero calls out to his or her partner "cover my back," we as Christians must learn to watch out for each other. Paul had the opportunity to allow others to watch his back many times. He had some opposition that wanted to see him stop his teaching and some of those wanted him dead! God reminded Paul that he had people to watch his back. God reminded Paul, "Don't be afraid, but keep on speaking and don't be silent. For I am with you, and no one will lay a hand on you to hurt you, because I have many people in this city" (Acts 18:9-10). ⑩ In Acts 9:25, Paul had the opportunity to appreciate his comrades' care for him while in Damascus when several of his associates lowered him one night in a basket through an opening in the city wall to protect him from those trying to kill him. Acts 23:12-22 reveals the story of Paul being arrested in Rome and some of his opposition swearing an oath to have him killed. Paul however benefited from friends who were watching his back, as he was warned of the opposition's plans and was able to get away.

⑩ What are two examples of people "having Paul's back" in situations other than Corinth?

Today, when we're putting a team together, we generally don't have to worry about murder plots. We do however have other potentially hostile acts that we have to deal with: a negative reputation from others at school and/or work; people who feel threatened by the message of Jesus Christ; or even legal threats from those with other "religious" views. We need to be on guard for and with one another as we learn to take a stand for the message of Christ.

Unfortunately, one of the most dangerous things we need to watch for is people in our own churches. Many times people whom we feel we should be able to trust the most are the ones who take cheap shots at us. The most difficult divisions come when started from within the church. Teenagers aren't immune to these difficulties. When peers argue and disagree, many times the entire group "takes sides" and gossip, slurs, and names fly. We must be on guard against the slander of each other. Only churches that work with one another, instead of against one another, will be able to thrive and become a truly contagious Christian community, that gets things done and draws others into a relationship with Christ.

SMALL-GROUP TIME: After presenting the teaching material, ask students to divide back into groups and discuss the "Do What?" questions. Small-group facilitators should lead the discussions and set the model for being open and honest in responding to questions.

Do What? (15 minutes)

Making It Personal

1. How did God choose to use a decree by Claudius that all Jews must leave Rome to His (God's) glory? What is God doing in your life now that is bringing Him glory?

2. What was significant when Paul "shook out his clothes" when the Jewish religious leaders became verbally abusive? How could you learn from this action of Paul? Who most opposes the message of Christ in your life?

3. When have you had a chance to experience a close community with a group of believers working together on the same goal, mission, or project? What memories do you have about that time? What do you remember most vividly? What contributed most to you growing closer as a team?

Small-group facilitators should reinforce the "LifePoint" for this session, making sure that students' questions are invited and addressed honestly.

LifePoint Review

Working together helps Christians grow.

"Do" Points

These "Do" Points will help you begin to experience this week's "LifePoint." Be open and honest as you discuss the action points within your small group.

1. Participate in one project or mission your church is involved in. Take time to get to know what your church is involved in. Find something to be involved in where you will find yourself using the talents God has given you and where others are using their talents as well. Make sure it is something you really care about, not just something you are doing out of obligation. Take the time to get to know others who work with you. How well do you contribute to the team?

2. Recognize the work someone else is doing and give them encouragement for their hard work. This is your chance to find someone else and cheer them on. One thing about team sports—you always are told to cheer on your teammates. Find a way to bring out the best in someone else by heartily cheering them on as they volunteer their time and energy.

3. Find a way to "protect" someone in your church who works hard at a position that makes them susceptible to the scrutiny of others. If others are criticizing someone, find a way to speak up for him or her and offer them encouragement. Don't let this person be criticized while you stand around—speak up. Pray for him or her. Do what is right to help this person know he or she is not alone.

Encourage students to list prayer needs for others in their books so they can pray for one another during the week.

Assign a student coordinator in each small group to gather the group's requests and e-mail them to the group members.

Prayer Connection:

This is the time to encourage, support, and pray for each other in our journeys to trust God and seek out real and personal encounters with Him.

Share prayer needs and requests with the group, especially those related to hearing from and responding to God. Your group facilitator will close your time in prayer.

Prayer Needs:

Encourage students to dig a little deeper by completing a "Now What?" assignment before the next time you meet.

Remind students about the "Get Ready" short daily Bible readings and related questions at the beginning of session 7.

Now What?

Remind them again this week that they are loved!

Deepen your understanding of who God is and His desire for us to have an authentic Christian community while we work together as a team, and continue the journey you've begun today by choosing one of the following assignments to complete this week:

Option #1:

If you enjoy writing, take the time this week to write a "Game Plan" for a team you are either on or desire to be on in your church. Try to think about the different people who will be needed to make this team successful. Do you need someone who is physically strong? Do you need those who are mentally strong? If possible, present your thoughts to an adult leader and if needed, organize your team.

Option #2:

Take some time this week and list all of the "teams" you know of in your church. Take the time to ask some questions of adults you know, and you will begin to realize that many teams already exist—some you might have never heard of. After you make your list, spend time praying for the teams in your church. Consider how you might become a part of one of these teams.

Bible Reference Notes

Use these notes to gain further understanding of the text as you study on your own.

1 Corinthians 3:9

we are God's co-workers. There are two basic ways of translating this phrase, both of which add to its understanding. The NRSV reads, "we are God's servants, working together." This points out that our work is in service to God and focuses on how we work together with other Christians on behalf of God. The NIV reads, "we are God's fellow workers," which is similar to the HCSB "God's co-workers," which pictures us working side by side with God Himself, doing God's work.
God's field, God's building. This refers to the Corinthian church, but the implication is that all who work for Jesus Christ are God's co-workers.

Acts 18:2

Aquila, Priscilla. This couple who apparently converted in Rome prior to meeting Paul, became important co-workers with him (v. 26; Rom. 16:3; 1 Cor. 16:19; 2 Tim. 4:19).
Claudius had ordered all the Jews to leave Rome. This is corroborated by the Roman historian Suetonius who wrote that the emperor, in A.D. 49, made this order because of uprisings in the Jewish community at Rome because of the influence of a man named *Chrestus,* which sounds like the Greek word for Christ. By the early 40s, riots broke out in the Jewish community in Rome between those who believed in Jesus as the Messiah and those who did not. To solve the problem, the emperor simply ordered all Jews to leave.

Acts 18:3

tentmakers. Rabbis were not paid for their teaching, so Paul would have had a trade even in his pre-Christian days as a Pharisaic rabbi.

Acts 18:6

shook out his clothes. Typically, Jews entering Palestine from a Gentile area wiped off their feet as a symbol of cleansing themselves from any traces of Gentile contamination picked up before entering the Holy Land. Thus, they would not share in God's judgment when He poured out His wrath upon the Gentile's land. Paul adapted this gesture to indicate that he was exempt from the judgment to come upon the Jews at Corinth.

Acts 18:7-8

Having left the synagogue, Paul made the house next door to it the center of his activity. Since Romans typically had three names, Titius Justus may be the Gaius whose home was the meeting place of the church (Rom. 16:23; 1 Cor. 1:14). It must have been galling enough for Paul to be teaching next to the synagogue in a home of a former synagogue member, but tensions undoubtedly became worse when Crispus, the synagogue ruler, professed faith as well (1 Cor. 1:14).

Acts 18:10

I am with you. This is the ultimate promise of God's protection found in similar Old Testament passages and on the lips of Jesus elsewhere (Matt. 28:20; John 14:18-21).

Session

7 FORGIVING ONE ANOTHER

Connections Prep

MAIN "LIFEPOINT": Forgiveness is necessary as we learn to be like Christ.

To reinforce the "LifePoint," leaders and small-group facilitators should understand the following more detailed CheckPoints and "Do" Points.

BIBLE STUDY CHECKPOINTS:

- Recognize the importance of forgiveness in building a contagious community.
- Look at the relationship between ungodly anger and our difficulties with forgiving one another.
- Recognize how the Holy Spirit both brings us together in unity and gives us the power to forgive.

LIFE CHANGE "DO" POINTS:

- Choose one person who has wounded you and pray for him or her each day this week.
- Work on healthy ways to channel your anger.
- Write a letter to someone with whom you are no longer in contact and with whom you are still angry.

PREPARATION:

- ☐ Review the leader book for this session and prepare your teaching in advance.
- ☐ Determine how you will divide students into small discussion groups.
- ☐ Recruit mature students or adults as small-group facilitators. Be sure these facilitators plan to attend your meeting.

REQUIRED SUPPLIES:

- ☐ *Contagious Community: Living Beyond Yourself* leader book for each group facilitator
- ☐ *Contagious Community: Living Beyond Yourself* student book for each student
- ☐ Pen or pencil for each student

"Get Ready" is primarily for students, but leaders and facilitators will benefit from these devotionals as well.

Get Ready

Read one of these short Bible passages each day, and spend a few minutes of focused time with God. Be sure to jot down any insights you receive.

MONDAY

Read Ephesians 4:25.
Are you a truthful person? Why? With whom do you have a tendency to "stretch the truth"? Who knows the real you?

TUESDAY

Read Ephesians 4:26.
When you get angry what do you do? How do you feel about the way you handle your anger? How has your anger caused you to sin?

WEDNESDAY

Read Ephesians 4:26-27.
Have you ever chosen to let your anger fester within you? What happened when you chose to do that? Is there someone in your life you are still angry at who you need to forgive? How can you do that?

THURSDAY

Read Ephesians 4:28.
What are you doing with the money you earn? Are you sharing your money or stuff with others? Do you know someone in need? How could you help someone in need today?

FRIDAY

Read Ephesians 4:29-30.

When you look back over the past 24 hours, have your words been used to hurt others or build them up? How? How could you choose to use your words differently?

SATURDAY

Read Ephesians 4:31.

Do you have any old anger? What is it from? Could you let it go? How could you work toward letting go of any old anger?

SUNDAY

Read Ephesians 4:32.

When you became a Christian, how much did God have to forgive you of? Were you guilty of just a few sins so you only needed a little forgiveness, or did you require all of God's forgiveness? How could you thank God for what He has forgiven you for? Take time to say thanks to God today if you have experienced His forgiveness.

7

LARGE-GROUP OPENING:
Get everyone's attention. Make announcements. Open the session with a prayer. Read the "LifePoint" to students.

LifePoint

Forgiveness is necessary as we learn to be like Christ.

SMALL-GROUP TIME: Instruct students to separate into groups of four to eight, preferably in a circle configuration. Call on the mature student or adult leaders you recruited to facilitate each small group through this "Say What?" segment.

Say What? (15 minutes)

Random Question(s) of the Week:

What is the weirdest thing you have ever eaten? Why did you eat it? Would you eat it again?

Group Experience: Do-Overs

Share the following questions with students in your small group and allow each student to answer. Encourage students to share their answers to the questions. The purpose of this experience is to allow students to share their thoughts with the group and also begin thinking about the groups with whom they spend their time.

1. In what activities do you most need a "do-over":
   - ☐ Hitting a baseball or softball (I need more than three strikes!)
   - ☐ Playing a piece of music (guitar, piano, and so forth)
   - ☐ Trying to cook
   - ☐ Homework/tests
   - ☐ Building something
   - ☐ Other ______________________________

2. If you were able to redo any part of your life, what part would you like to have a chance to do over?

3. What cartoon characters from your younger days are most in need of a remake? How would you remake them? Would you change their superhero powers or just update them?

LARGE-GROUP TIME: Direct students to turn to face the front for this teaching time. Be sure you can make eye contact with each student in the room. Encourage them to follow along and take notes in their student books.

Share the "So What?" information with students. You may modify it to meet your needs. Be sure to highlight the underlined information, which gives answers to the student book questions and fill-in-the-blanks (shown in the margins).

So What? (30 minutes)

Teaching Outline

I. The Treasure of Forgiveness
- A. Jesus' sacrifice
- B. Sin's damage

II. Learning from the Bible
Ephesians 4:25-32

III. Managing Anger
- A. Using it for protection
- B. Using it as a weapon

IV. Building Each Other Up

V. Honoring the Holy Spirit
Maintain unity

The Treasure of Forgiveness

Ernest Hemingway wrote a beautiful story about a Spanish father who decided to reconcile with his son who had run away to Madrid. The regretful father took out an ad in a Madrid newspaper that read: *Paco, meet me at Hotel Montana Tuesday, all is forgiven—Papa.* Since Paco is a common name in Spain, when the father went to the hotel, he found 800 young men named Paco waiting for their fathers. This is an incredible picture of forgiveness! Can you imagine the scene? While Hemingway was not a Christian, he has drawn for us a picture that perfectly describes the cries of so many for one thing—the forgiveness of their fathers. Today, that story is still as true as it was then. Many people desperately want forgiveness and ultimately to be reconciled to others. Guilt, however, sticks deep inside us and forms a wedge between forgiveness and us; we long to be free of guilt and its irritation. Forgiveness is an amazing treasure that brings freedom, but like many treasures, it is not easily found. A contagious community is a community where freedom and healing can be found.

❶ What are two vital clues Scripture gives us about finding God's forgiveness?

❶ <u>Scripture has two vital clues about finding the treasure of forgiveness. (1) The first is that forgiveness enters our world through the sacrifice that Jesus made.</u> This

❷ Why is it not enough to simply say, "I'm sorry" to find God's forgiveness? What else needs to happen?

is closely related to our ability to accept God's forgiveness. Some people are looking for an easy forgiveness; one that says "I'm sorry," then all is forgiven and things go back to the way they were before. But sin can't be swept under the rug. ❷ Sin creates damage that we cannot repair. Our harsh words and actions put scars on others both physically and emotionally. When we lie to others, we damage their trust in us. As a result, our sin creates damage between God and us. The damage we do through sin requires more than a simple "I'm sorry." Hebrews 9:22 states, "without the shedding of blood there is no forgiveness." Jesus gave much more than we could ever imagine to help remove sin, and He opened the door to the treasure that is God's forgiveness. (2) The second is that in order to be forgiven, we need to be willing to forgive. In Matthew 6:14-15, Jesus stated, "For if you forgive people their wrongdoing, your heavenly Father will forgive you as well. But if you don't forgive people, your Father will not forgive your wrongdoing."

❸ Where is the center for contagious forgiveness?

We must understand that forgiveness is contagious. When we have the courage to forgive others who have hurt us, forgiveness spreads to those within our Christian community with whom we come in contact. ❸ The center for this contagious forgiveness is God Himself. He forgave us, then instructed us to forgive each other.

While most people see the value of forgiveness, it might be one of the hardest things many of us are asked to do. It's not that difficult if all someone did was show up late for a movie or eat the last piece of pizza, but other times forgiveness is more difficult to give. What about the times when someone destroys something of yours, lies to you, gossips about you, or even physically hurts you? In these cases, forgiveness is much more difficult to give.

Today, our culture is full of reasons not to forgive someone else. Even the late president John F. Kennedy is credited with saying, "Forgive your enemies, but never forget their names." We watch movies like *Rambo* and find ourselves rooting for the good guy to get revenge on the bad guys. We read literature, like *Romeo and Juliet,* which ends tragically due to the inability of two feuding families to find forgiveness. These all tend to shape us to withhold forgiveness from others until they earn it. Reading or watching these stories that portray so vividly how deeply people can be hurt and how hard forgiveness can be, lays out our own challenge even more directly. The good news is that people can learn to forgive and in that forgiveness comes healing.

Before the session, enlist a youth to read Ephesians 4:25-32.

Learning from the Bible

25 Since you put away lying, Speak the truth, each one to his neighbor, because we are members of one another. 26 Be angry and do not sin. Don't let the sun go down on your anger, 27 and don't give the Devil an opportunity. 28 The thief must no longer steal. Instead, he must do honest work with his own hands, so that he has something to share with anyone in need. 29 No rotten talk should come from your mouth, but only what is good for the building up of someone in need, in order to give grace to those who hear. 30 And don't grieve God's Holy Spirit, who sealed you for the day of redemption. 31 All bitterness, anger and wrath, insult and slander must be removed from you, along with all wickedness. 32 And be kind and compassionate to one another, forgiving one another, just as God also forgave you in Christ.

Managing Anger

One important key to forgiveness is how we manage our anger. Some people manage their anger by not really managing it at all—they just let it out. This creates more damage and hurt. Others, however, choose to stuff their anger down inside themselves and pretend like it doesn't exist. They are the ones who forgive, but never forget. They are the ones who can say a heart-felt, "I forgive you," and years later are able to recount the hurtful event with exact details.

❹ What are two purposes for the emotion of anger that God gave us?

Paul addressed anger in our focal passage. First, he wrote, "Be angry and do not sin" (v. 26). It's important to note that this statement does not prohibit or condemn anger. Rather, it assumes it will happen! That's right, we need to come to grips with the fact that we are going to get angry. God made us with many emotions, and He gave each one of them to us with a purpose. ❹ Our anger is both a natural protection, just like the needles of a porcupine or shell of a turtle, and a weapon to be used against the wrongs of this world. When Jesus saw the Pharisees with hypocritical hearts or the commercial greed of the money changers in the temple, he got angry. When the people of Israel worshipped idols, God got angry. Since God made us in His image, should we not also be upset when God's people don't act like Him?

❺ What are three examples of expressing anger in a sinful way?

The point is not that we need to avoid the feeling of anger—it's given to us by God—but we must avoid our anger causing us to sin. ❺ Sinful behavior involves striking out in anger and causing more damage. It's saying hateful words that damage or kill another person's spirit. It's making sure we let the other person, "know what they did to you" by trying to hurt him or her like he or she hurt us—also known as revenge.

We are called to work on restoring the relationships we have through honest, timely communication. The communication has to be honest, and it must express our feelings ("speak the truth" with our neighbor, v. 25), as well as have a goal of a prompt resolution of the conflict. Paul states in verse 26, "Don't let the sun go down on your anger." When we hold on to our anger for days at a time, it has the chance to deeply embed in our lives. The anger begins to take over our feelings and thoughts, and forgiveness becomes more difficult to give.

Building Each Other Up

❻ What does Scripture state about the way we should and should not use words when we are angry?

Forgiveness also requires us to act positively toward the one who wronged us. We can't offer forgiveness with gritted teeth or with a scowl on our face. We must show an effort to build up the other person and the relationship. ❻ In verse 29 we are told, "No rotten talk should come from your mouth, but only what is good for the building up of someone in need, in order to give grace to those who hear." "Rotten talk" does not refer to using foul language, but rather talk that would tear down someone else. James 3:9-10 states, "With [the tongue] we bless our Lord and Father, and with it we curse men who are made in God's likeness. Out of the same mouth come blessing and cursing. My brothers, these things should not be this way." Rather, we should think of our words as a vital repair tool. They are the needle and thread to repair the hole in someone's clothes, not the sharp knife that rips away and produces the hole. They are the pump that puts air in the deflated tire, not a nail that causes the air to leak out so the tire goes flat.

Forgiving someone is not easy. Forgiveness requires us to evaluate the relationship we have with the other person and forces us to discuss and resolve the conflict or problem. We might also have to realize that the other person had legitimate good intentions with their actions, even though we were offended or hurt. Or we might have to realize that the other person was frustrated with something (possibly us) when they reacted to us the way they did. We must look for ways to help build others up and help resolve conflict. It might seem strange to consider building someone up when they are down, frustrated, or angry, but it is exactly what God has called us to do. In verse 32 Paul reminds us that we are to be "forgiving one another, just as God also forgave you in Christ." God responded to our hurts and rejection of Him by sending His Son, Jesus, to bring us healing and hope. We can offer the same message of hope and forgiveness to others as we learn to follow His steps.

Honoring the Holy Spirit

❼ Why is an unwillingness to forgive a brother or sister an offense against the Holy Spirit?

Forgiveness ultimately means we must maintain the unity with each other that the Holy Spirit desires us to have. ❼ It is God's will for us to be a united family, and when we are not, it "grieves the Holy Spirit" (v. 30). Paul tells us in 1 Corinthians 12:13, "For we were all baptized by one Spirit into one body—whether Jews or Greeks, whether slaves or free—and we were all made to drink of one Spirit." Then, in Ephesians 4:3, Paul stated that we are to be "diligently keeping the unity of the Spirit with the peace that binds us." So when we don't forgive our brother or sister, it's not just an offense against him or her, but it's an offense against the Holy Spirit who wants to bind us together. Choosing not to forgive someone is us saying to the Holy Spirit, "What you want is not important to me! I choose revenge!" How can we turn our backs on the Holy Spirit's prompting and still claim to follow Him?

We should not, however, choose to view the Holy Spirit as a guilt producer; rather, we must understand that the Holy Spirit is the power of God that allows us to have unity and reconciliation to others. He seeks to bring us together, not create feelings of inadequacy with others. He is our most valuable resource in finding what it takes to forgive in difficult situations. When we struggle to find the ability to forgive others, regardless of how they have hurt us, we should pray for the Spirit's power and ability to bring us together with them and experience forgiveness. The Holy Spirit has been bringing those who oppose each other together for centuries—Jews and Gentiles, slaves and masters, political enemies, and today—rival schools and sports teams. The Holy Spirit can do the same for you in your relationships today! We just need to ask and not grieve the Holy Spirit by our resistance to act as we are prompted.

SMALL-GROUP TIME:
After presenting the teaching material, ask students to divide back into small groups and discuss the "Do What?" questions. Small-group facilitators should lead the discussions and set the model for being open and honest in responding to questions.

Do What? (15 minutes)

Making It Personal

1. How did God choose to use a decree by Claudius that all Jews must leave Rome to His glory? What is God doing in your life now that is bringing Him glory?

2. What was significant when Paul "shook out his clothes" when the Jewish religious leaders became verbally abusive? How could you learn from this action of Paul? Who most opposes the message of Christ in your life?

3. When have you had a chance to experience a close community with a group of believers working together on the same goal, mission, or project? What memories do you have about that time? What do you remember most vividly? What contributed most to your growing closer as a "team"?

Small-group facilitators should reinforce the "LifePoint" for this session, making sure that students' questions are invited and addressed honestly.

LifePoint Review

Forgiveness is necessary as we learn to be like Christ.

"Do" Points

These "Do" Points will help you begin to experience this week's "LifePoint." Be open and honest as you discuss the action points within your small group.

1. <u>Choose one person who has wounded you and pray for him or her each day this week.</u> We have all been there. Someone has hurt us, and we have chosen to focus more on our anger than loving that person. This week think of one person who has hurt you and pray for them when you think of them, when you are angry with them, when you get mad at them, and when you see them. You will find God doing an amazing work in your life as you lift them up to Him.

2. <u>Work on healthy ways to channel your anger.</u> Everyone gets angry, that's true, but how you take that anger out has a great affect on yourself and others. This week concentrate on recognizing the times when you are angry and consciously find other ways to get rid of your anger without blowing your top. Maybe you could try journaling, blogging, reading your Bible, exercising, or talking with a friend. Take the time to explain and understand your anger and explain what you would like to happen to resolve your anger.

3. <u>Write a letter to someone with whom you are no longer in contact and with whom you are still angry.</u> Whether the person lives out of state, has passed away, or you simply lost contact with them, take the time to put your thoughts, emotions and feelings into a letter to them. Let them know how you feel toward them and why. After you write the letter, seal it, then pray and ask the Holy Spirit to help you forgive him or her. Afterward you might bury it, burn it, or put it somewhere where you can read it again in a year or two to see how you have grown.

Encourage students to list prayer needs for others in their books so they can pray for one another during the week.

Assign a student coordinator in each small group to gather the group's requests and e-mail them to the group members.

Prayer Connection:

This is the time to encourage, support, and pray for each other in our journeys to trust God and seek out real and personal encounters with Him.

Share prayer needs and requests with the group, especially those related to hearing from and responding to God. Your group facilitator will close your time in prayer.

Prayer Needs:

Encourage students to dig a little deeper by completing a "Now What?" assignment before the next time you meet.

Remind students about the "Get Ready" short daily Bible readings and related questions at the beginning of session 8.

Now What?

Remind them again this week that they are loved!

Deepen your understanding of who God is and His desire for us to have an authentic Christian community while we work together as a team, and continue the journey you've begun today by choosing one of the following assignments to complete this week.

Option #1:

Make a list of all of the things that make you angry. Create your own "pet peeve" list. This week as you experience one of these "pets" take the time to not only recognize it but also write it down. As you compile your list during the week, take time each day to pray for the person(s) who committed these acts that caused you to get angry. Then look at your own life. What have you done this week that might cause someone else to be angry with you? Create a list of ways you can be more responsible with your own actions to keep from angering others.

Option #2:

Take some time this week and rewrite Ephesians 4:25-31 in your own words. Feel free to paraphrase the passage or rewrite it in paragraph form. The important thing is to grasp and communicate the meaning of the passage. Be prepared to share your thoughts next week with your small group.

Bible Reference Notes

Use these notes to gain further understanding of the text as you study on your own.

Ephesians 4:25

Since. This verse is a model for how Paul discussed each of six topics. He began with the negative deed, in this case, "lying." (In Greek, the word is literally *the lie.*) Then he sets in contrast the positive virtue that he commends, in this case, truthful speech. Then he gives the reason for the command. Here the reason is that we are all neighbors. In fact, we are even closer than that—"we are all members of one another." Lies destroy fellowship. Unity must be built on trust, and trust comes via truth.

Ephesians 4:26

Be angry. Paul recognizes there is such a thing as legitimate anger. He wrote in 5:6 that God experiences anger, though the translation obscures the meaning. (Although the phrase in 5:6 is rendered as "God's wrath," the same word is used there, which is here translated "anger.") Jesus was angry (Mark 3:5). There are certain situations in which anger is the only honest response. For Christians to deny their anger is dangerous and self-defeating. But once admitted, anger is to be dealt with, and so Paul gives four instructions relating to expressing anger. First, do not sin. The sin is not being angry, but rather expressing it in a destructive way by seeking to injure or destroy the person with whom you are angry. Second, don't let the sun go down on your anger. That is, deal with it quickly. Don't nurse anger and let it grow. Third, don't let anger develop into resentment. This is what the word translated "anger" at the end of verse 26 means. Get the anger out in the open. Be reconciled if possible. Apologize if it is appropriate. Fourth, don't give the Devil an opportunity. Don't let Satan exploit your anger, turning it into hostility or using it to disrupt fellowship.

Ephesians 4:28

It is not enough simply to stop stealing; the thief must also start working.

Ephesians 4:29-30

From the use of one's hands, Paul turns to the use of one's mouth. The word translated "rotten" is used to describe spoiled fruit. Instead of rancid words that wound others, the words of Christians ought to edify ("building up"), be appropriate ("of someone in need"), bring grace ("give grace"), and not cause distress for the Holy Spirit (by unholy words).

Ephesians 4:31

Paul identified six negative expressions of anger that must be erased from the Christian life.
bitterness. Spiteful, long-standing resentment.
anger and wrath. These two attitudes are related. The first is anger that is out of control in terms of how it is expressed; the second is a more long-term, sullen hostility, where unexpressed anger has been allowed to grow, in violation of what Paul said in verse 26.
insult. Anger expressed with an intent to destroy their reputation.
slander. Anger expressed through verbal abuse.
wickedness. Wishing or plotting evil against another.

Ephesians 4:32

In contrast to the negative attitudes listed in verse 31, Paul identified a set of positive attitudes that ought to characterize the Christian. Instead of those negative expressions of anger, the Christian ought to be kind, compassionate, and forgiving.

notes

7

Notes

Session

8 BEING GENEROUS WITH ONE ANOTHER

Connections Prep

MAIN "LIFEPOINT": We are like Christ when we give to others.

To reinforce the "LifePoint," leaders and small-group facilitators should understand the following more detailed CheckPoints and "Do" Points.

BIBLE STUDY CHECKPOINTS:

- Understand why Paul claims giving to God and others is a privilege.
- Appreciate how giving contributes to unity in the community.
- Consider how generosity starts with giving ourselves to God and each other.

LIFE CHANGE "DO" POINTS:

- Dedicate (or rededicate) yourself to serving Jesus Christ as Lord and Savior.
- Make a pledge of time that you will spend giving to others.
- Give financially to God and His work.

8

PREPARATION:

- ☐ Review the leader book for this session and prepare your teaching in advance.
- ☐ Determine how you will divide students into small discussion groups.
- ☐ Recruit mature students or adults as small-group facilitators. Be sure these facilitators plan to attend your meeting.

REQUIRED SUPPLIES:

- ☐ *Contagious Community: Living Beyond Yourself* leader book for each group facilitator
- ☐ *Contagious Community: Living Beyond Yourself* student book for each student
- ☐ Pen or pencil for each student

"Get Ready" is primarily for students, but leaders and facilitators will benefit from these devotionals as well.

Get Ready

Read one of these short Bible passages each day, and spend a few minutes of focused time with God. Be sure to jot down any insights you receive.

MONDAY

Read 2 Corinthians 8:1.

Do you know what God is doing around you? How can you make yourself more aware of what God is doing in your community, your state, the nation, and the world?

TUESDAY

Read 2 Corinthians 8:2.

When you think about giving, what comes to mind? What can you give other than your money? When have you ever been generous with someone else? Did you give out of your excess or did you give out of your own poverty and hardship?

WEDNESDAY

Read 2 Corinthians 8:3-4.

How do you feel about giving to God's work? Is it a privilege or an obligation that Christians have to do? What could you do to make giving more meaningful?

THURSDAY

Read 2 Corinthians 8:5.

Have you given yourself completely to God? If so, when? If not, why? Are you living like you have or have not?

FRIDAY

Read 2 Corinthians 8:6-7.

Would you say you excel at giving? What could you do to be a better giver?

SATURDAY

Read 2 Corinthians 8:8-10.

When it comes to giving, do you look at what others give? Do you limit giving to just money? Should you compare yourself to others or Christ? What has Jesus Christ given you?

SUNDAY

Read 2 Corinthians 8:11-15.

How much of your time and energy are you willing to give so that God's work gets done? How will you use your time, talent, and treasures to help God's work be done?

LARGE-GROUP OPENING:
Get everyone's attention. Make announcements. Open your session with a prayer. Read the "LifePoint" to students.

LifePoint

We are like Christ when we give to others.

SMALL-GROUP TIME:
Instruct students to separate into groups of four to eight, preferably in a circle configuration.

Call on the mature student or adult leaders you recruited to facilitate each small group through this "Say What?" segment.

Say What? (15 minutes)

Random Question(s) of the Week:
Where were you six hours ago? What were you doing?

Group Experience: "Money" Questions
Share the following questions with the students in your small group and allow each student to answer. Encourage students to share their answers to the questions. The purpose of this experience is to allow students to share their thoughts with the group and also begin thinking about the groups with whom they spend their time.

1. What is your attitude about money?
   - ☐ Money is the root of all evil.
   - ☐ Show me the money!
   - ☐ I want something, and I'll get it; money is no object.
   - ☐ A penny saved is a penny earned.
   - ☐ You can't buy happiness, but you sure can rent it!
   - ☐ Here today, gone tomorrow.
   - ☐ What's money? Is that what they used before credit cards?
   - ☐ The best things in life are free!
   - ☐ Other ____________

2. If someone suddenly gave you $50,000, what would you do with it? Be honest.

3. What has your family taught you about money? Do you feel equipped to survive on your own with your current financial knowledge? How can your church help prepare you?

LARGE-GROUP TIME:

Direct students to turn to face the front for this teaching time. Be sure you can make eye contact with each student in the room. Encourage them to follow along and take notes in their student books.

Share the "So What?" information with students. You may modify it to meet your needs. Be sure to highlight the underlined information, which gives answers to the student book questions and fill-in-the-blanks (shown in the margins).

So What? (30 minutes)

Teaching Outline

I. Understanding Giving

II. Learning from the Bible
2 Corinthians 8:1-15

III. Giving as a Privilege

IV. Giving as a Sign of Love

V. Giving and Unity in the Body

Understanding Giving

❶ What three different kinds of giving does Paul refer to in the focal passage?

When we hear the word *generous* we often think about our money. That isn't always the case though. In our focal passage from 2 Corinthians, ❶ Paul referred to three kinds of giving: (1) Giving self to God. This is where it started for the Macedonians (v. 5), and it is where it should start for us. If we have not given ourselves fully over to God, then no other giving makes sense to us. It seems foolish, but when we give ourselves first to God, we see our giving as serving God and God's children. (2) Giving self to those around us. Paul wrote that after the Macedonians gave themselves to God they gave themselves "to us by God's will." In other words, they realized that being part of a caring community is God's will; (3) Giving all of our resources (time, talent, finances, and so forth) to God and God's children in need—only after we give ourselves to God and give ourselves to others.

❷ What was the purpose of the offerings Paul worked so hard to raise?

We must understand that in our world the need for money for a church to operate is a reality. In our churches we must pay bills just like everyone else. Since we are called to minister to and care for people in need, money is a necessity for a church. However this is not something that is new. It goes back to the time of Paul. ❷ Paul worked hard to raise money to help with the poor people of the Jerusalem church. Acts 11:27-30 states that a famine spread "throughout the Roman world." Apparently, it hit particularly hard in Jerusalem because verses 29-30 state, "So each of the disciples, according to his ability, determined to send relief to the brothers who lived in Judea. This they did, sending it to the elders by means of Barnabas and Saul."

8

❸ What children's story teaches essentially the same thing that Paul teaches in this passage about giving and community?

So how can a teenager be generous in his or her church? ❸ The classic children's story, "Stone Soup," is a great example. In the story, a couple of hungry travelers come to a town where they hope someone will share their food with them. But the townspeople are stingy and choose to hide their food. The travelers decide it's time to make "stone soup." They claim that by putting a stone in water, they can make a delicious, nutritious soup. The townspeople are of course skeptical, but fascinated with the thought. As the "soup" cooks, the travelers talk about how much better stone soup is when other ingredients—onions, potatoes, and beef—are added to it. With each item they mention, someone relents and admits he or she has some of the item and puts it in the soup. Soon, of course, they have a delicious soup. The story teaches us a wonderful lesson—life can be so much more of a feast when we loosen up and share what we have.

Much like stone soup, our churches will benefit when teenagers add their own unique ingredients. Churches need more than money from teenagers; they need someone who might be willing to lend a hand, help others in need, and share generously with all of what "little" we might have. Some might say that "Stone Soup," while a good

❹ What two things is Paul saying in this passage?

story for children, is naïve when it comes to dealing with the real world. ❹ But Paul wouldn't have said so, because essentially he expressed the same message—(1) we need to have a community in which all share generously and (2) in which everyone benefits.

Before the session, enlist a youth to read 2 Corinthians 8:1-15.

Learning from the Bible

1 We want you to know, brothers, about the grace of God granted to the churches of
Macedonia: 2 during a severe testing by affliction, their abundance of joy and their
deep poverty overflowed into the wealth of their generosity. 3 I testify that, on their
own, according to their ability and beyond their ability, 4 they begged us insistently for
the privilege of sharing in the ministry to the saints, 5 and not just as we had hoped.
Instead, they gave themselves especially to the Lord, then to us by God's will. 6 So we
urged Titus that, just as he had begun, so he should also complete this grace to you.
7 Now as you excel in everything—in faith, in speech, in knowledge, in all diligence, and
in your love for us—excel also in this grace.

8 I am not saying this as a command. Rather, by means of the diligence of others,
I am testing the genuineness of your love. 9 For you know the grace of our Lord Jesus
Christ: although He was rich, for your sake He became poor, so that by His poverty you
might become rich. 10 Now I am giving an opinion on this because it is profitable for
you, who a year ago began not only to do something but also to desire it. 11 But now
finish the task as well, that just as there was eagerness to desire it, so there may also
be a completion from what you have. 12 For if the eagerness is there, it is acceptable
according to what one has, not according to what he does not have. 13 It is not that
there may be relief for others and hardship for you, but it is a question of equality—
14 at the present time your surplus is available for their need, so that their abundance
may also become available for your need, that there may be equality. 15 As it is written:

> ***The person who gathered much did not have too much,***
> ***and the person who gathered little did not have too little.***

Giving as a Privilege

We must learn to look at giving as a privilege rather than an obligation. As teenagers we can't view giving in the same way we look at Christmas. In other words, we can't be on the lookout for what we are going to receive; rather, we must understand that we have an opportunity to give to others.

❺ How does Paul describe giving as a motive rather than as a guilt trip?

Paul wrote how the Macedonians, "begged us insistently for the privilege of sharing in the ministry of the saints" (v. 4). Did they consider giving to be a privilege? ❺ Many of us associate appeals to giving with guilt trips that almost assault us with pictures of starving children or comparisons between our relatively lavish lifestyle and the need of those in a third world country. Paul however referred to a relatively poor and struggling community that saw giving as a privilege. They realized it was a privilege because their contributions would make them full-fledged members of a team doing the work of Christ. If a football player who has sat on the bench for most of the season is suddenly given a starting position on the team, he doesn't refer to the *obligation* of having to go play, rather, he considers it a *privilege* to start and contribute to the team.

Some teenagers view their talents and gifts as insignificant to the larger church. They don't see the need to invest in the church, because they see themselves as a lesser part. This is completely untrue. We must understand that even as teenagers we are investing in others' lives with all of our resources—not just our finances. ❻ Jesus, in the Sermon on the Mount, declared, "Don't collect for yourselves treasures on earth, where moth and rust destroy and where thieves break in and steal. But collect for yourselves treasures in heaven, where neither moth nor rust destroys, and where thieves don't break in and steal. For where your treasure is, there your heart will be also" (Matt. 6:19-21). Jesus was thus declaring the kingdom of heaven to be something we must invest in, and the Macedonians in our passage were wanting to be a part of it.

❻ How does Jesus encourage us to invest in the kingdom of heaven?

Giving as a Sign of Love

If giving were only a privilege, however, it would almost seem self focused: "Give because of how you will benefit from it." If we are talking about how giving strengthens a community, we need to see that it reaches far beyond self focus. We must understand that giving away something that has no value to us is simple. If we choose to give away something that means a great deal to us (our favorite shirt to a friend who needs it, our time to help someone study, or the money for the cup of coffee at the local coffee shop to someone who is hungry) we begin to understand that our giving is motivated by our love for God and others.

8

Giving is an indicator of whether or not love is genuine. Paul stated this exact thing when he told the Corinthians that in checking out their willingness to give to this offering he was "testing the genuineness of your love" (v. 8). Love that is real is shown by giving—giving away part of us to help others know Christ. ❼ God showed His love for us by giving us His Son, and He calls us to show that our love is genuine in the same way—we must be willing to give away what is important to us to see others know Christ. John wrote in 1 John 3:17, "If anyone has this world's goods and sees his brother in need but shuts off his compassion from him—how can God's love reside in Him?"

❼ What do we learn about showing love through God's giving of His Son?

❽ Our culture has taught us two things that we must correct if we are to become a contagious community—(1) love is easy to talk about and (2) work hard to

❽ What two things has the world taught us about giving?

❾ What must we do to correct these thoughts?

accumulate "stuff." ❾ We must learn to counter these by learning not to just talk about love but show it to others, and we must learn to see opportunities to show our love to others by being generous with our possessions.

Giving and Unity in the Body

❿ What is the connection between giving and unity in a community?

❿ Giving is also a definite way to declare our unity with each other. It's saying that your needs are my needs. After Paul encouraged the Corinthians to give to the offering for the poor in Jerusalem, he wrote, "it is not that there may be relief for others and hardship for you, but it is a question of equality—at the present time your surplus is available for their need, so that their abundance may also become available for your need, that there may be equality" (vv. 13-14). The idea was that a community is established where no one says that the other person's needs is none of their concern. If we are all one in Christ, then, as Paul wrote in 1 Corinthians 12:26, "if one member suffers, all the members suffer with it; if one member is honored, all the members rejoice with it." When we are truly as sensitive to the needs of others as we are to our own needs, then we are truly one in Christ.

SMALL-GROUP TIME: After presenting the teaching material, ask students to divide back into small groups and discuss the "Do What?" questions. Small-group facilitators should lead the discussions and set the model for being open and honest in responding to questions.

Do What? (15 minutes)

Making It Personal

1. What is the connection between giving ourselves to the Lord (v. 5) and giving our resources to help with the needs of others?

2. How did Paul use the terms "rich" and "poor" in verse 9? How do we become "rich" through Christ's "poverty"?

3. What do you need to do at this point in your life in order to be more like the generous Macedonians and less like the more hesitant Corinthians?

Small-group facilitators should reinforce the "LifePoint" for this session, making sure that students' questions are invited and addressed honestly.

LifePoint Review

We are like Christ when we give to others.

"Do" Points

These "Do" Points will help you begin to experience this week's "LifePoint." Be open and honest as you discuss the action points within your small group. Here are some actions to help you understand more about biblical giving:

1. <u>Dedicate (or rededicate) yourself to serving Jesus Christ as Lord and Savior.</u> Talk to someone you trust (church staff member, deacon, Sunday School teacher, parent) about your choice to serve Christ. If you have already made a public profession of faith in Christ, this is like a rededication. This is a time to share your heart with someone else and allow them to keep you accountable for your choice to follow Christ with your whole life.

2. <u>Give financially to God and His work.</u> Giving is not just about finances, but when we give financially we are contributing to help others by allowing ministries and organizations to get resources to carry out God's work. You might not have a job yet, but don't let that stop you. Next time you have the choice to go grab a cup of coffee with friends after school, download some new songs, or see a movie, think about giving that money to God's work instead of spending it. It's tough to admit how much money we spend on ourselves when we claim not to have anything to give to God's work.

3. <u>Make a pledge of time that you will spend giving to others.</u> Many people are willing to give financially to support the church, but would you be willing to set aside a portion of your time each week to serve others? Would you be willing to miss some television viewing time, hang-out time, or time with friends to help serve others. You can serve others through your church, a peer-study time, working with an after-school program for younger kids, or other ways. Find a way to give up your time to help someone else.

Encourage students to list prayer needs for others in their books so they can pray for one another during the week.

Assign a student coordinator in each small group to gather the requests and e-mail them to the group members.

Prayer Connection:

This is the time to encourage, support, and pray for each other in our journeys to trust God and seek out real and personal encounters with Him.

Share prayer needs and requests with the group, especially those related to hearing from and responding to God. Your group facilitator will close your time in prayer.

Prayer Needs:

Encourage students to dig a little deeper by completing a "Now What?" assignment before the next time you meet.

Remind students about the "Get Ready" short daily Bible readings and related questions at the beginning of session 9.

Now What?

Remind them again this week that they are loved!

Deepen your understanding of who God is and His desire for us to have an authentic Christian community while we understand how our finances impact the world for Christ, and continue the journey you've begun today by choosing one of the following assignments to complete this week:

Option #1:

This week as you watch television, make a list of 10 commercials that have caught your eye. Explain what the commercial was for, what it was selling, and how you felt after watching the commercial. Did the commercial persuade you to consider giving up your money in order to get the product available? Create your own commercial for giving money to church. It can either be funny or serious.

Option #2:

Take some time this week and keep track of all the money you spend and where you spend your time. Total the money up by these categories: necessities, wants, stuff you didn't need. Total your time up by categories: things you had to do, things you wanted to do, things you wish you hadn't done. After you total the amount of money and time you spent, spend time asking God to help you best serve Him with your generosity. Write a prayer to God regarding your finances and time. Share that prayer with others when you meet as a group.

Bible Reference Notes

Use these notes to gain further understanding of the text as you study on your own:

2 Corinthians 8:1

churches of Macedonia. Macedonia was the Roman province just north of the province of Achaia where Corinth was located. The churches in mind were probably those located at Philippi, Thessalonica, and Berea (Acts 16:6–17:15).

2 Corinthians 8:2

a severe testing by affliction. Paul referred back in 7:5 to being "afflicted in every way" while in Macedonia. In Acts, we are told that Paul was flogged and imprisoned at Philippi (16:22-24), and rioted against in Thessalonica (17:5-9), as well as in Berea (17:13-15). The churches in these areas had then grown up in a hostile atmosphere.
deep poverty. In general, most Christians of this time were poor, but these were evidently more so than others were.

2 Corinthians 8:4

This verse contains three words that show how the motivation for this offering sprang not only from humanitarian concerns, but from distinctly Christian convictions as well.
privilege. Literally, *grace.*
sharing. The Greek word is koinonia, often translated as *fellowship.* Giving is an expression of partnership in Christ.
ministry. Giving is a way of ministering to the needs of others, a Christian responsibility.

2 Corinthians 8:7

Paul exhorted the Corinthians to participate in giving as wholeheartedly as they participated in the exercise of other spiritual gifts (1 Cor. 12:7-11; 14:1) and as a reflection of their desire to affirm his apostleship (7:11).

2 Corinthians 8:11

now finish the task. This is reminiscent of Christ's parable of the two sons, one who said he was going to do something (work in the vineyard), but didn't, and the other who said he would not, but did (Matt. 21:28-32). Following through on good intentions is vital.
from what you have. One reason the Corinthians may have stalled is that they felt they could not make a significant contribution. The question is not how much one gives, but simply that one gives out of love for God and people.

2 Corinthians 8:13

equality. In their abundance, the Corinthians were to share what they had with those who were in need. Likewise, in the future, it could be the other way around, and the Corinthians could expect aid if they needed it from Christians in Jerusalem and elsewhere.

Notes

Session

9 TEACHING ONE ANOTHER

Connections Prep

MAIN "LIFEPOINT": As we understand our faith, we have a responsibility to teach others.

To reinforce the "LifePoint," leaders and small-group facilitators should understand the following more detailed CheckPoints and "Do" Points.

BIBLE STUDY CHECKPOINTS:

- Study the role of teaching and learning in developing a contagious Christian community.
- Learn from Paul, Priscilla, and Aquila, and how they taught others in the early church.
- Understand why being a continual learner is important to developing our faith.

LIFE CHANGE "DO" POINTS:

- Set personal learning goals for the next year.
- Seek a mentor relationship where learning is a priority.
- Outline three things you have learned about your relationship with Christ during the previous year.

PREPARATION:

- ☐ Review the leader book for this session and prepare your teaching in advance.
- ☐ Determine how you will divide students into small discussion groups.
- ☐ Recruit mature students or adults as small-group facilitators. Be sure these facilitators plan to attend your meeting.

REQUIRED SUPPLIES:

- ☐ *Contagious Community: Living Beyond Yourself* leader book for each group facilitator
- ☐ *Contagious Community: Living Beyond Yourself* student book for each student
- ☐ Pen or pencil for each student

"Get Ready" is primarily for students, but leaders and facilitators will benefit from these devotionals as well.

Get Ready

Read one of these short Bible passages each day, and spend a few minutes of focused time with God. Be sure to jot down any insights you receive.

MONDAY

Read Acts 18:18-19.
What was significant about Paul engaging in discussion with the Jews in the synagogue? What do you think was the attitude of the Jewish leaders toward Paul?

TUESDAY

Read Acts 18:20-23.
How much time are you investing in building others up? How could you change your current practices to spend more time purposefully building others up?

WEDNESDAY

Read Acts 18:24.
How would you describe your knowledge of Scripture? Are you satisfied with your current knowledge of Scripture? What benefits could you have if you increased your knowledge of Scripture?

THURSDAY

Read Acts 18:25-26.
What subject are you most knowledgeable about? How do you react to correction? How do you react to correction about your knowledge of Scripture? Have you ever been questioned about your knowledge of Scripture? Why or why not?

FRIDAY

Read Acts 18:27-28.
Who is someone who has stood behind you when you chose to stand up for something? How did you react to their support? Have you thanked them for their support?

SATURDAY

Read Colossians 3:16.
How richly does the message of Christ dwell within you? How are you showing that outwardly?

SUNDAY

Read Colossians 3:16.
When have you purposefully taught others what you know about Christ? With whom are you sharing wisdom, singing, and gratitude?

LARGE-GROUP OPENING:
Get everyone's attention. Make announcements. Open your session with a prayer. Read the "LifePoint" to students.

LifePoint

As we understand our faith, we have a responsibility to teach others.

SMALL-GROUP TIME:
Instruct students to separate into groups of four to eight, preferably in a circle configuration.

Call on the mature student or adult leaders you recruited to facilitate each small group through this "Say What?" segment.

Say What? (15 minutes)

Random Question(s) of the Week:

When did you last change clothes? Why?

Group Experience: Learning

Share the following questions with the students in your small group and allow each student to answer. Encourage students to share their answers to the questions. The purpose of this experience is to allow students to share their thoughts with the group and also begin thinking about the groups with whom they spend their time.

1. What is your attitude about learning?
   - ☐ I can't learn enough . . . give me more!
   - ☐ I can't wait to be out of school!
   - ☐ I learn what I want when I want to.
   - ☐ I might not understand it right now, but I'm sure I'll need it one day, so I choose to learn everything I can.
   - ☐ I am full of useful information.

- ☐ I don't understand why I need to learn this. I'm not going to use it later in life.
- ☐ Why can't learning be optional?
- ☐ Who's bright idea was "school" anyway?
- ☐ Other ____________

2. Who is your favorite teacher of all time? Why?

3. What is your favorite subject to study? Why?

So What? (30 minutes)

LARGE-GROUP TIME: Direct students to turn to face the front for this teaching time. Be sure you can make eye contact with each student in the room. Encourage them to follow along and take notes in their student books.

Share the "So What?" information with students. You may modify it to meet your needs. Be sure to highlight the underlined information, which gives answers to the student book questions and fill-in-the-blanks (shown in the margins).

Teaching Outline

I. Everyone Teaches

A. Learn from each other
B. Share what you've learned

II. Learning from the Bible

A. Colossians 3:16
B. Acts 18:18-28

III. A Richer Faith

A. Look past the obvious
B. Know Christ more
C. Continuous journey

IV. A Stronger Faith

A. Tragedy
B. Persecution

V. An Accurate Faith

A. What you believe
B. Why you believe it

Everyone Teaches

After the group experience, say something like, "many of us think about learning and have a negative attitude. God does not want us to quit learning, rather, He wants us to continue to learn and teach others. In our focal passage this session, Paul had his hair cut, not to experiment or to experience the latest fashion, but to fulfill a vow. In essence, he wanted to show how seriously he took discipleship, teaching, and learning about Christ. Today we will look at the role teaching and learning play in a contagious Christian community."

As you begin your teaching of the lesson, make it a point to yawn. Yawn big and dramatic, then say something like, "Wow, that yawn felt great!" Then look around and notice as students react. Some will yawn themselves while others will suppress their own yawn. The point is that students realize that a yawn is contagious. As you teach, make mention of a yawn being a teaching point of how we can show others how we feel. Some will yawn when they simply hear the word, others when they see someone yawn, and others will try your "experiment" when they leave your meeting.

❶ Why is being a Christian teacher considered a high calling?

Teachers are important in our culture today, just as they were in Jesus' day. Today no one has more influence over a child outside the home than teachers. Teachers shape the dreams and desires of many children. If a child's teacher is good, then it's natural that a child might want to be like his or her teacher. ❶ In the New International Version of the Bible, Jesus is referred to as "teacher" 46 times in the Gospels. In John 13:13 of the Holman Christian Standard Bible, Jesus says, "You call Me Teacher and Lord. This is well said, for I am." For Christians who seek to be like Jesus there is no higher calling. James, however, cautions people against taking on this high calling: "Not many should become teachers, my brothers, knowing that we will receive a stricter judgment" (3:1).

In spite of the cautions of being labeled a Christian teacher, we all need to be teaching those around us. We all have information, skills, and knowledge that we can pass on to others. We must realize that we all have something to offer others. As a teenager, you must recognize you are forming who you are and how you will live. As you do this, you are learning from others, whether you are doing so purposefully or not. You must work purposefully to grasp knowledge about Christ and the Christian life before you can teach others what you know.

❷ As Christians, what two things do we need in order to learn for our sake and be able to teach others for the good of the Kingdom?

❷ As Christians, what we need is the spirit of grace and humility that allows us to both learn and teach. Sometimes people love to teach because they like the feeling of "being in the know" in front of others. Some teach to boost their egos and enjoy the "respect" they get from others. These attitudes however can also make it difficult to learn from others. These "non-teachable" personalities also make it difficult for prospective learners to desire to be a part of the learning process as well. Many people love to learn, but don't have the confidence to pass their learning along to others. While we each have our gifts, and some have the specific spiritual gift of teaching and some do not, ❸ a true community needs to be one in which we can all learn from each other, and we can all share what we have learned.

❸ What two things happen in a true Christian community?

While we must guard against teaching to serve our egos and selfish desires, legitimate benefits abound from teaching others. ❹ Legitimate benefits one might seek from teaching are: the satisfaction that comes from helping someone reach his or her highest potential, the satisfaction of using teaching talents for God, and the more intimate relationship that results when we share the learning venture with someone else. These benefits not only help the teacher but also greatly benefit the learner. Today we will focus on the benefits of Christian teaching in the early church.

❹ What are three legitimate benefits a teacher might seek for him- or herself?

Before the session, enlist a youth to read Colossians 3:16 and Acts 18:18-28.

Learning from the Bible

16 Let the message about the Messiah dwell richly among you, teaching and admonishing one another in all wisdom, and singing psalms, hymns, and spiritual songs, with gratitude in your hearts to God.

18 So Paul, having stayed on for many days, said good-bye to the brothers and sailed
away to Syria. Priscilla and Aquila were with him. He shaved his head at Cenchreae,
because he had taken a vow. 19 When they reached Ephesus he left them there, but he
himself entered the synagogue and engaged in discussion with the Jews. 20 And though
they asked him to stay for a longer time, he declined, 21 but said good-bye and stated,
"I'll come back to you again, if God wills." Then he set sail from Ephesus.
22 On landing at Caesarea, he went up and greeted the church, and went down to
Antioch. 23 He set out, traveling through one place after another in the Galatian territory
and Phrygia, strengthening all the disciples.
24 A Jew named Apollos, a native Alexandrian, an eloquent man who was powerful in
the Scriptures, arrived in Ephesus. 25 This man had been instructed in the way of the
Lord; and being fervent in spirit, he spoke and taught the things about Jesus accurately,
although he knew only John's baptism. 26 He began to speak boldly in the synagogue.
After Priscilla and Aquila heard him, they took him home and explained the way of
God to him more accurately. 27 When he wanted to cross over to Achaia, the brothers
wrote to the disciples urging them to welcome him. After he arrived, he greatly helped
those who had believed through grace. 28 For he vigorously refuted the Jews in public,
demonstrating through the Scriptures that Jesus is the Messiah.

A Richer Faith

The learner benefits from a good teacher by developing a richer faith. Paul told the Colossians in 3:16 to, "Let the message about the Messiah dwell richly among you."

❺ What are four things Christian faith brings us besides salvation from hell?

The phrase, "dwell richly" suggests getting past a mere surface understanding of the faith and discovering the fullness of what Christ and the gospel is all about. Paul was challenging those who heard his message to look beyond what many today call "fire insurance" or a "get out of hell" opportunity. Is that true? Yes! But faith in Christ is so much more. He was challenging his learners as well as us today to look past the obvious and know Christ more. ❺ The Christian faith is also a way of confronting physical needs and bringing people together (Matt. 25:31-46; Acts 2:42-47); it's a way of seeing how the universe is connected (Col. 1:5-20); a way to understand the direction of human history (Rev. 21:1-5); and a way to understand what this life is all about (Matt. 6:25-34; 16:24-26) to name just a few things. Paul challenges learners today to not just wade into the "shallow waters" of faith, but to dive "deep" into the ocean of who Christ is. Many have compared the Christian life to a foot race, and it is often referred to an endurance or "distance" race where stamina and patience play a key role, rather than to a sprint, where speed and quickness are the keys to victory. Faith in Christ is more than a stand-alone, single event; rather it is a journey that we are on continuously. It was this same rich faith that prompted the seeker Jews of Ephesus to want more time to spend with Paul. They could tell this new way of looking at faith would take some time to absorb. It is this rich faith that can be found in the foundations of any contagious Christian community.

A Stronger Faith

❻ What were two reasons why it was important for Christians to strengthen each other in Paul's day?

As a learner in Christ, you also benefit from developing a stronger faith that can be advantageous and help you make it through hard times. In our focal passage from Acts, we learn in verse 23 that Paul went "traveling through one place after another in the Galatian territory and Phrygia, strengthening all the disciples." ❻ At the time, this was especially necessary because Christians were facing various kinds of opposition, even harassment. This harassment included being ridiculed from Jewish religious leaders, who considered Christianity to be blasphemous, and Gentile business leaders, who saw their faith as a threat to their business interests (Acts 16:16-24; 19:23-41). They needed a faith that would help them during times of ridicule and opposition. In addition, they lived in a hard world where people died much younger than they do today, and where tragedy was an even more possible occurrence. They needed a strong faith that would help them make some sense of such traumatic happenings in their lives.

What these disciples needed, we also need today. We are not immune to harassment and ridicule ourselves. Around the globe more and more Christians face persecution for their beliefs. More and more communities are becoming "closed" to the gospel globally. Many colleges and universities today ridicule and laugh at those who go against or question scientific theories or claim belief in an "Intelligent Design" (or

❼ What are five difficult circumstances we face today?

God-created earth). ❼ While life is not as hard as it might have been in Paul's day, we still face many difficult circumstances; we have loved ones battling with cancer; AIDS has spread throughout the world and infects many in our society; we battle terrorism, kidnappings, and violence. We need a strong faith that will help us face such tragic forces in our society. When we teach others the depth of the Christian faith, we help them develop a faith that will weather all the storms life can throw at us. We benefit from this ourselves as we pass on what we have personally experienced from our own faith in Christ.

An Accurate Faith

Dealing with difficult circumstances is not the only threat to our faith today. We also must face the threat of those who challenge what we believe and try to tear us away from it. We need a faith that can withstand such attacks and accusations. We need to know what we believe and why we believe it. We must develop spiritual ownership of our lives. We can no longer live on the faith of our parents, grandparents, or churches. We must actively know Christ and what He taught. Acts tells us of how Priscilla and Aquila taught Apollos "the way of God to him more accurately" (v. 26). Specifically, they taught him because "he knew only John's baptism" (v. 25). ❽ John had baptized Jews to symbolize repentance and spiritual cleansing (Acts 19:4). Christian baptism means that and much more. It symbolizes Christ's death and resurrection (Rom. 6:1-10), and it means we have chosen to be identified with the community of faith. While not all Christian denominations baptize the same way, Scripture nonetheless affirms that we have "one Lord, one faith, one baptism" (Eph. 4:5).

❽ How was Christian baptism different from the baptism of John?

This "correction" of Apollos' knowledge was important because Apollos needed to know the difference between the baptism of John and the baptism of those who followed Jesus just as there was a difference between the community of John the Baptist and the community of Christ. The community of John the Baptist was based completely around repentance and mourning the immoral past of Israel—petitioning God for forgiveness and pleading for mercy. The community of Christ however was built around a forgiveness found only in Christ and a promise of hope for the future. This is an example of how doctrinal issues really do matter and how it is important at times to attend to them.

It is important as a teenager for you to understand the importance of both knowing God's Word and being taught by someone who knows God's Word deeply. When you study God's Word, you deepen your understanding of who God is and what His desires are for you. When you sit under someone else's teaching, you gather that person's wisdom and knowledge as well. You must learn from Apollos' attitude in regard to Priscilla and Aquila. When we read about this couple in Scripture, we find that Priscilla's name is usually mentioned first. This was against the cultural norm of the day. Many scholars today view this as an indication of Priscilla's status and influence in the community. Apollos benefited greatly from his willingness to listen to and apply the teaching of someone else to his life.

Also, as a teenager, you must come to understand that no one has all of the answers. That's right, no one. There are some subjects that have caused theologians and philosophers to debate viciously over for years. You do not have to have a definitive answer to these questions. What you must have is an accurate knowledge of the faith in Christ that will help you as you talk about, discuss, and share your faith with others. Paul shared with Timothy in 1 Timothy 4:12, "No one should despise your youth; instead, you should be an example to the believers in speech, in conduct, in love, in faith, in purity." Many teenagers across the world have read that verse and been challenged by it. You too, can have a knowledge and wisdom about the things of God that challenges others.

SMALL-GROUP TIME:
After presenting the teaching material, ask students to divide back into small groups and discuss the "Do What?" questions. Small-group facilitators should lead the discussions and set the model for being open and honest in responding to questions.

Do What? (15 minutes)

Making It Personal

1. How does Paul's reception by the Jews of Ephesus seem to differ from his reception by Jews elsewhere? *(Example: Acts 17:8)*

2. Why is it significant that Priscilla and Aquila took Apollos to their home to instruct him "more accurately" (Acts 18:26)? How could this have aided his willingness to receive their correction? What can you learn from this?

3. Who in this story do you need to be more like?
   - ☐ Paul—willing to go out of my way to strengthen others
   - ☐ "the Jews" (Acts 18:19-20)—to be hungry to learn more
   - ☐ Priscilla and Aquila—to learn tact in teaching others
   - ☐ Priscilla and Aquila—to be willing to teach others
   - ☐ Apollos—to have a more thorough knowledge of Scripture
   - ☐ Apollos—to be more open about receiving correction
   - ☐ Other ________________________________

Small-group facilitators should reinforce the "LifePoint" for this session, making sure that students' questions are invited and addressed honestly.

LifePoint Review

As we understand our faith, we have a responsibility to teach others.

"Do" Points

These "Do" Points will help you begin to experience this week's "LifePoint." Be open and honest as you discuss the action points within your small group. Here are some actions to help you understand more about biblical giving:

1. Set personal learning goals for the next year. You don't have to wait for January 1 to set goals for the next 365 days. Set goals that will bring you closer to Christ. These might include reading a certain number of chapters in the Bible daily, attending Bible studies regularly, or taking a class offered by your church.

2. Seek a mentor relationship where learning is a priority. You can connect with someone older (of the same sex) who can walk through your Christian life with you. This person can aid you as you seek to meet your goals (stated above), as you seek to know Christ more, and can keep you accountable on a regular basis. This person should have a relationship with Christ that you have seen evidence of, whom you desire to be more like.

3. Outline three things you have learned about your relationship with Christ during the previous year. These things can be simple or profound, but they should be things that you have learned over the previous year. Purpose to find a way to pass on the wisdom you have gained to others in the coming days.

Encourage students to list prayer needs for others in their books so they can pray for one another during the week.

Assign a student coordinator in each small group to gather the group's requests and e-mail them to the group members.

Prayer Connection:

This is the time to encourage, support, and pray for each other in our journeys to trust God and seek out real and personal encounters with Him.

Share prayer needs and requests with the group, especially those related to hearing from and responding to God. Your group facilitator will close your time in prayer.

Prayer Needs:

Encourage students to dig a little deeper by completing a "Now What?" assignment before the next time you meet. Remind students about the "Get Ready" short daily Bible readings and related questions at the beginning of session 10.

Now What?

Remind them again this week that they are loved!

Deepen your understanding of who God is and His desire for us to teach and learn from one another, and continue the journey you've begun today by choosing one of the following assignments to complete this week:

Option #1:

Keep a journal of your week, paying special attention to times when you are instructed. Have you taken the instruction you have received to heart, or have you simply allowed it to enter into one ear and seep out the other? How well do you handle instruction? Make note of how you feel when someone else is teaching. How would you prefer to be instructed?

Option #2:

Write a letter to a respected adult, asking for instruction. This letter doesn't have to be mailed or sent, rather the purpose is for you to understand where you are lacking in your own personal knowledge. No one becomes a mature Christian overnight, rather it takes years on the journey we call faith. Whom would you pick to write your letter to? Why? What is keeping you from asking this person for his or her help?

Bible Reference Notes

Use these notes to gain further understanding of the text as you study on your own:

Colossians 3:16

the message about the Messiah. While certain false teachers had lost connection with Christ as head of the church (Col. 2:8), the message the Colossians taught one another must be centered on Jesus (2:19).

dwell richly among you. This is a form of the word for *fullness*. Spiritual fullness is rooted neither in secret knowledge nor in mystical experiences but in a commitment to Christ.

teaching . . . singing. Rather than referring to two distinct activities (teaching and singing), Paul is referring to worship services where the people shared their knowledge of God through singing to one another.

psalms, hymns, and spiritual songs. The psalms are the Old Testament Psalms. Hymns were songs common to the church. (Examples may be Luke 1:46-55, 1:68-79; John 1:1-18; Eph. 5:14; Phil. 2:6-11; Rev. 4:11) Spiritual songs were spontaneous expressions of praise to Christ.

Acts 18:18

Priscilla and Aquila were with him. It is significant that Priscilla's name is listed first, ahead of her husband. This was hardly ever done, and probably indicates that Priscilla was the more influential leader of the two.

he shaved his head . . . because he had taken a vow. Pious Jews would take vows based on the pattern of the Nazirites (Num. 6:1-21), as an indication of their devotion to God. Since the cutting of one's hair indicated the termination of the vow, Paul may have made a vow of dedication to God for as long as he was in Corinth in gratefulness to God's promise of protection (Acts 18:10). While normally vows would be terminated by shaving one's head and offering a sacrifice in the temple at Jerusalem, people far from the city could shave their heads where they were and carry the trimmings to the temple to be presented along with a sacrifice. Luke may have included this incident as evidence that Paul did not abandon the traditions of his people.

Cenchreae. A port city near Corinth (Rom. 16:1).

Acts 18:19-21

The positive response to Paul among the Jews at Ephesus sets the stage for his return to that city in 19:1. Priscilla and Aquila stayed on at Ephesus and established the new church there.

Acts 18:19

the Jews. Paul and many of his team were Jews, but Acts generally uses this term for the Jewish religious leaders of the day. This was one of the rare times when the Jewish establishment showed a genuine interest in what Paul was teaching about the Messiah.

Acts 18:22-23

Because of his vow, Paul undoubtedly went to Jerusalem to offer a thank offering. Then he proceeded to Antioch, the church that had spawned his missionary work in the first place (13:1-3). He may have stayed there until the spring (A.D. 52 or 53), when traveling would again be possible. From there he visited the churches throughout the area where he had established churches on his first trip (13:13–14:20).

Acts 18:22

strengthening all the disciples. Paul was not the kind of evangelist who was only interested in saving souls in order to put notches on his spiritual belt. He was also very careful to come back to them to nurture them along the way (14:21-22).

Acts 18:24-28

During Paul's journey, Apollos visited Ephesus. While Apollos is a minor figure in Acts (nothing more is said of him after 19:1), he was a significant figure in the church at Corinth and became a valued associate of Paul's (1 Cor. 1:12; 3:4-23; 4:6; 16:12; perhaps 2 Cor. 8:22). Some modern scholars, following Luther, wondered if he might have authored Hebrews. This incident, as well as that in 19:1-7, shows that Acts records only a small part of the story of how the gospel was spread throughout the known world. While their stories are not recorded, the other apostles, as well as many unknown believers, played important roles in spreading the story of Jesus far beyond Judea.

Session

10 LIVING AT PEACE WITH ONE ANOTHER

Connections Prep

MAIN "LIFEPOINT": We must choose to be peaceful.

To reinforce the "LifePoint," leaders and small-group facilitators should understand the following more detailed CheckPoints and "Do" Points.

BIBLE STUDY CHECKPOINTS:

- Understand how Jesus tore down the dividing wall of hostility between Jews and Gentiles.
- Understand and choose to follow Christ's call to be at peace with one another.
- Look at how we can choose to be reconciled to God and others.

LIFE CHANGE "DO" POINTS:

- Offer a gesture of peace to someone with whom you have been fighting or arguing.
- Be an influence of peace in your Christian community.
- Go out of your way to bring peace to someone you have overlooked.

PREPARATION:

- ☐ Review the leader book for this session and prepare your teaching in advance.
- ☐ Determine how you will divide students into small discussion groups.
- ☐ Recruit mature students or adults as small-group facilitators. Be sure these facilitators plan to attend your meeting.

REQUIRED SUPPLIES:

- ☐ *Contagious Community: Living Beyond Yourself* leader book for each group facilitator
- ☐ *Contagious Community: Living Beyond Yourself* student book for each student
- ☐ Pen or pencil for each student

"Get Ready" is primarily for students, but leaders and facilitators will benefit from these devotionals as well.

Get Ready

Read one of these short Bible passages each day, and spend a few minutes of focused time with God. Be sure to jot down any insights you receive.

MONDAY

Read Mark 9:50.
Why do you think this passage compares you to "salt"? How are you like salt to those around you? What are the benefits of being like salt to others? How can having salt "among yourselves" bring peace?

TUESDAY

Read Ephesians 2:11-12.
How much hope would you say you have in your life right now? What would give you more hope?

WEDNESDAY

Read Ephesians 2:13-14.
How has Christ brought you together with someone whom you might have previously been at odds? How is your relationship with that person now?

THURSDAY

Read Ephesians 2:15-16.
How have your relationships with others been affected by God's grace? Have they benefited from God's grace? How could you be more responsive to God's grace in relationship with others?

FRIDAY

Read Ephesians 2:17-20.

When you have been a stranger, how do you feel? When you feel out of place, how can Jesus help you feel connected again?

SATURDAY

Read Ephesians 2:21-22.

How would you act or react if you knew that God was always within you and with you? What do you need to change immediately?

SUNDAY

Read John 14:27.

How does having peace inside you relate to having peace with others?

LARGE-GROUP OPENING: **Get everyone's attention. Make announcements. Open your session with a prayer. Read the "LifePoint" to students.**

LifePoint

We must choose to be peaceful.

SMALL-GROUP TIME: **Instruct students to divide into groups of four to eight, preferably in a circle configuration.**

Call on the mature student or adult leaders you recruited to facilitate each small group through this "Say What?" segment.

Say What? (15 minutes)

Random Question(s) of the Week:

What was the last thing you bought? Was it worth it? Would you buy it again?

Group Experience: Strangers

Share the following questions with the students in your small group and allow each student to answer. Encourage students to share their answers to the questions. The purpose of this experience is to allow students to share their thoughts with the group and also begin thinking about the groups with whom they spend their time.

1. What is the attitude in your house toward strangers?
   - ☐ There are no strangers here; only friends we haven't met yet!
   - ☐ Don't talk to strangers.
   - ☐ You never know, a stranger could be an angel in disguise.
   - ☐ Even your best friend was once a stranger.
   - ☐ Stick with your own kind, strangers bring trouble.
   - ☐ Other ______________________________

2. Describe a situation when you felt like a stranger. Why did you feel "out of the loop"? How did you react?

3. If you were going somewhere and knew you would be a stranger, how would you like to be welcomed? What would need to happen in order for you to no longer feel like a stranger?

LARGE-GROUP TIME: **Direct students to turn to face the front for this teaching time. Be sure you can make eye contact with each student in the room. Encourage them to follow along and take notes in their student books.**

Share the "So What?" information with students. You may modify it to meet your needs. Be sure to highlight the underlined information, which gives answers to the student book questions and fill-in-the-blanks (shown in the margins).

So What? (30 minutes)

Teaching Outline

I. Seeking Peace

A. Influence your world

B. Preserve what is right and wrong

II. Learning from the Bible

A. Mark 9:50

B. Ephesians 2:11-12

III. An Inclusive Community

Equal access

IV. A Reconciled Community

A. To God

B. To each other

V. A Family of Faith

Show the peace of Christ to the world

Seeking Peace

When we talk about peace, we normally are talking about the absence of war. When you think of peace, do flowers and anti-war statements come to mind? We desire for peace in Iraq, Afghanistan, Europe, or some other "hot spot" of turmoil. That kind of desire for peace is important for us to desire, but for true peace to happen it needs to start on a personal level with us. We need to live in harmony with those in our own city, neighborhood, and church. We especially need to learn to live at peace with those within our church, since that is part of our witness to both our city and neighborhood.

❶ What is the full meaning of the Hebrew word, "Shalom"?

❶ It is significant that the Hebrew word for peace, Shalom, means far more than simply the absence of conflict. It means a sense of shared harmony and well-being. It embodies the kind of peace that Christ calls us to have with each other. He instructs us in Mark 9:50 to "have salt among yourselves and be at peace with one another." The "salt" part of that verse might seem a little out of touch with us today. However, when we realize the importance of salt in Jesus' culture, we understand what He is saying more clearly. Salt was a highly valued commodity in Jesus' day. Not only was it important as a flavor for food as today, but in an age without refrigeration, it was also a preservative. ❷ Therefore, Christ seems to have been calling His followers to influence (flavor) their world, as well as to preserve what was right and good. Certainly, doing both of these things helps to maintain peace and harmony between people.

❷ What did Christ mean when He told His followers to "have salt among yourselves" (Mark 9:50)?

❸ Why is it important to maintain peace in the church?

❸ Maintaining peace with one another in the church is an important witness to a world that has too many walls and divisions. Yet, as anyone knows who has spent much time inside the church, that is not very easy to do. In the local church, members fight over everything from what color to paint a particular wall to who gets the closest parking spaces. These disagreements aren't void from teenage groups either. While the arguments might not be over wall color or parking spaces, teenagers tend to argue and fight over popularity, where to go as a group, and who should or should not be included. Teenagers outside the church world see Christians acting like everyone else—fighting and arguing amongst themselves—and can't see a benefit to a relationship with Christ.

While having a peaceful relationship with others is difficult, a relationship with Christ dictates that we are to "be at peace with one another," and Paul spoke of

Jesus tearing down "the dividing wall of hostility" (Ephesians 2:14). While perfect agreement in a world of so many complex issues might be too much to expect, can we afford to disregard the call to be at peace with one another? In this session, we will discuss this question and consider what it means to live at peace with one another in a redemptive community of faith.

Before the session, enlist a youth to read Mark 9:50 and Ephesians 2:11-22.

Learning from the Bible

50 "Salt is good, but if the salt should lose its flavor, how can you make it salty? Have salt among yourselves and be at peace with one another."

11 So then, remember that at one time you were Gentiles in the flesh—called "the uncircumcised" by those called "the circumcised," done by hand in the flesh. 12 At that time you were without the Messiah, excluded from the citizenship of Israel, and foreigners to the covenants of the promise, with no hope and without God in the world. 13 But now in Christ Jesus, you who were far away have been brought near by the blood of the Messiah. 14 For He is our peace, who made both groups one and tore down the dividing wall of hostility. In His flesh, 15 He did away with the law of the commandments in regulations, so that He might create in Himself one new man from the two, resulting in peace. 16 He did this so that He might reconcile both to God in one body through the cross and put the hostility to death by it. 17 When Christ came, He proclaimed the good news of peace to you who were far away and peace to those who were near. 18 For through Him we both have access by one Spirit to the Father. 19 So then you are no longer foreigners and strangers, but fellow citizens with the saints, and members of God's household, 20 built on the foundation of the apostles and prophets, with Christ Jesus Himself as the cornerstone. 21 The whole building is being fitted together in Him and is growing into a holy sanctuary in the Lord, 22 in whom you also are being built together for God's dwelling in the Spirit.

Walls have been around in communities throughout human history. In certain areas of Europe you can still find various towns that are still surrounded by walls just as they were in the Middle Ages. These walls protected the community from invaders and helped define the particular community. On the other hand, the strength of the wall was also its weakness. Its strength was that it kept out outsiders. Its weakness, ironically, was that it kept outsiders away. In a primitive society surrounded by hostile people, keeping outsiders out is a very good idea. However, for a society to progress it must be exposed to new ideas, and for peace between people to have a chance, opposing sides must be allowed to come together, let down the walls, and get to know one another. In such an atmosphere, a wall is a huge hindrance. The Berlin Wall was a good example of a wall that was set up to separate people that really needed to come together.

❹ What are the "two sides" to walls?

❹ So, in a sense, walls figuratively—as well as literally—have two sides. They can offer protection from the outside, but they can also limit our ability to truly understand those outside. In a classic "Peanuts" cartoon, Linus is building a brick wall, and Sally says, "That's a nice wall, Linus. Is it supposed to keep things in or is it supposed to keep things out?" Linus pauses for a moment and says, "I don't know, it hasn't decided yet." That's the way it is with walls in our own lives; they can easily keep others out, but they can also just as easily keep us in.

❺ How did Christ tear down the "dividing walls of hostility" between the Jews and the Gentiles?

❺ The temple in Jerusalem had a wall that was supposed to keep out Gentiles. The purpose was to protect the purity of the faith. But at the same time, it walled out people to whom the nation of Israel should have been a light (Isa. 49:6). Paul declared that Christ, by bringing together Jews and Gentiles under the same banner of grace, had torn down this "dividing wall of hostility" (Eph. 2:14). In doing so, Jesus made it possible for Jews and Gentiles to come together in one community, a community no longer divided by walls. Let's take a look at the nature of this new community.

An Inclusive Community

The community that Christ made possible was an inclusive community. The community of Israel had been an exclusive community up until this point. The Gentiles were shut out. Paul mentioned this as he wrote to the Gentiles who made up the Ephesian church. "So then, remember that at one time you were Gentiles in the flesh—called 'the uncircumcised' by those called 'the circumcised,' done by hand in the flesh" (2:11). Circumcision was a sign done in the flesh to indicate that some—the Jews—were included in the community of God, while others—the Gentiles—were excluded from the family of God. Dr. Suess has a wonderful story about the Star-bellied Sneetches, who considered themselves better than Sneetches who didn't have a star on their bellies—that is, until someone came along who could put stars on the bellies of the other Sneetches and make them theoretically equal. In response, the Star-bellied Sneetches decided to remove the stars from their own bellies thus making starlessness the new sign of superiority within the Sneetch community!

In a sense, the Jewish men of Paul's time were the "Star-bellied Sneetches" of their day because they had the physical mark that separated them from others. To be fair, God had ordered the use of this practice in the law (Gen. 17:10; Lev. 12:3) to set them apart from the non-believers and keep them from being assimilated into the surrounding culture. Over time however, it changed from a symbol of being *different* to a symbol of being *better.*

Over time all of the law had become a rendition of the "star on the belly." The law was seen as the exclusive property of Israel, and it was the only way people could connect to God. That was why the Gentiles were, as verse 12 notes, seen as "without the Messiah, excluded from the citizenship of Israel, and foreigners to the covenants and promise, with no hope and without God in the world."

❻ How did Christ make the people of God become a more inclusive community?

❻ Paul was saying that in Christ the people of God had become an inclusive community. It was based on something to which all people had equal access—the grace of God in Jesus Christ. "For He is our peace, who made both groups one and tore down the dividing wall of hostility. In his flesh, He did away with the law of the commandments in regulations, so that He might create in Himself one new man from the two, resulting in peace" (vv. 14-15). Without the law, without the "star on the belly," all were on the same ground, and there was no longer a basis for division.

Today, as teenagers, the possibility to look at those outside the church as "incomplete" very much exists. We must be on our guard to make sure those inside the church don't begin to feel superior or more deserving of God's grace. We must remember it was a free gift to each of us, and is a free gift offered to everyone—regardless of background or nationality.

A Reconciled Community

Because of Christ, the Gentiles could not just be a part of an inclusive community; they could also be a part of a reconciled community. As Paul wrote in verse 13, "But now in Christ Jesus, you who were far away have been brought near by the blood of the Messiah." This new people of God could now be both reconciled to God and reconciled to each other. They could be reconciled to God through the sacrifice of Jesus Christ on the cross. Jesus died for the sins of Jews and Gentiles alike. No one can satisfy all the requirements of the Law not even the most faithful Jew. Paul wrote this perhaps more clearly than in any other place in Scripture. "For by grace you are saved through faith, and this is not from yourselves; it is God's gift—not from works, so that no one can boast" (2:8-9). So the Gentiles, who had once been without God and hope (v. 12), could have both.

❼ Name three leaders of the early church who were Jews and three leaders of the early church who were Gentiles.

This reconciliation, however, also includes reconciliation between people. Christ is all about tearing down the walls. This is a crucial point and very relevant to all of us today. ❼ The church Jesus established had both Jews like Paul, Peter, and James, and Gentiles like Luke, Timothy, and Stephen. Jews and Gentiles eating together and staying under the same roof went from being a scandalous rarity to the common practice of the faith community. A redemptive community today needs to be one where we are reconciled to both God and to each other.

A Family of Faith

Because of what God did in Christ, Jews and Gentiles were brought together into one family. Gentiles, for the first time, had the opportunity to join in the family of God. Paul, writing to the Gentiles of Ephesus, wrote, "So then you are no longer foreigners and strangers, but fellow citizens with the saints, and members of God's household" (v. 19).

It would be less than honest if we didn't acknowledge that while Christ made possible this new family and many have been reconciled as a result of Jesus, many others have tried to rebuild those walls. The record of Christian violence against Jews has been appalling. Even within the Christian faith, people have built walls between each other, between Catholics and Protestants, between denominations, and even between different factions of the same Christian denomination. That is hardly "living at peace with one another!" ❽ This demonstrates that we still have not fully realized the potential of what God has done in Christ. Christ calls us to peace without walls. We must respond in obedience and faith. To the degree that we do respond, we can be part of a community of peace that shows Christ's peace to the world.

❽ If Christ tore down the dividing wall of hostility between Jews and Gentiles, why do we still have tensions between these two groups?

SMALL-GROUP TIME: After presenting the teaching material, ask students to divide back into groups and discuss the "Do What?" questions. Small-group facilitators should lead the discussions and set the model for being open and honest in responding to questions.

Do What? (15 minutes)

Making It Personal

1. In today's Scripture passage, Paul referred to those who are "near" or "far away" (vv. 13,17). From whom are they "near" or "far away"?

2. What does our passage point to as the most effective tool in tearing down the "dividing wall of hostility" between Jews and Gentiles?

3. In order to tear down the dividing walls that exist in your life right now, what do you need to do next?

10

Small-group facilitators should reinforce the "LifePoint" for this session, making sure that students' questions are invited and addressed honestly.

LifePoint Review

We must choose to be peaceful.

"Do" Points

These "Do" Points will help you begin to experience this week's "LifePoint." Be open and honest as you discuss the action points within your small group. Here are some actions to help you understand more about living in peace with one another:

1. Offer a gesture of peace to someone with whom you have been fighting or arguing. If you have been arguing with someone, choose to make peace with him or her. It might be a parent with whom you have been arguing over doing your chores; if so, then do your chores without complaining. It might be a sibling to whom you have been showing disrespect; if so, choose to show them respect and not fight with them. Maybe it's a friend with whom you have had a disagreement and neither of you have chosen to seek peace; if so, find time to talk through your differences with the other person. Whatever you choose to do, make sure your motives are pure. Don't chose to do something in order to get your way, but do it as an attempt to bring peace with the other person and heal the relationship.

2. Be an influence of peace in your Christian community. Do you have friends who are in conflict with each other? Could you be a part of bringing peace to their relationship? Bring them together to discuss how to come to peace in their relationship. Find a place that is away from others, where you can help them come to a compromise. Watch and see how God's peace can heal relationships.

3. Go out of your way to bring peace to someone you have overlooked. Do you know someone in your school who is different? Do they look different, are they a different race or nationality, or are they just "different"? Find a way to get to know that person and get to know how they feel. You might find that they need peace in their lives because they feel overlooked on a regular basis. Pray and ask God to lead you to someone who needs to know His peace.

Encourage students to list prayer needs for others in their books so they can pray for one another during the week.

Assign a student coordinator in each small group to gather the group's requests and e-mail them to the group members.

Prayer Connection:

This is the time to encourage, support, and pray for each other in our journeys to trust God and seek out real and personal encounters with Him.

Share prayer needs and requests with the group, especially those related to hearing from and responding to God. Your group facilitator will close your time in prayer.

Prayer Needs:

Encourage students to dig a little deeper by completing a "Now What?" assignment before the next time you meet.

Remind students about the "Get Ready" short daily Bible readings and related questions at the beginning of session 11.

Now What?

Remind them again this week that they are loved!

Deepen your understanding of who God is and His desire for us to have an authentic Christian community while we understand our role in bringing peace to the world, and continue the journey you've begun today by choosing one of the following assignments to complete this week:

Option #1:

Keep a journal this week of the conflict that you see among your friends and peers. As you journal, make note of conflicts that involve you and others. Each day review the conflicts about which you have written. Write a prayer daily for each of these conflicts. Answer the following questions daily: How can God's peace bring an end to these conflicts? What is the root of these conflicts? How can you be a part of bringing peace to these conflicts?

Option #2:

Take time this week to look at the word "peace." Get out your Bible and a concordance and look up the word "peace" in the Bible. Pick 10 instances of the word "peace" in the Bible and write what you think the passage means. As you study about peace, write a plan for your life of how you will choose peace in your life.

Bible Reference Notes

Use these notes to gain further understanding of the text as you study on your own:

Mark 9:50

salt. Salt does not normally lose its taste, but salt from the Dead Sea was mixed with impurities and over time could acquire a stale taste. If Jesus' followers lose their "salt" (their witness, their ability to "bring flavor" to the world), this is not easily restored.
be at peace with one another. When Jesus' followers have a sense of witness and service, peace is the outcome.

Ephesians 2:11

remember. In 2:1-3, Paul reminded his Gentile readers that once they were trapped in their transgressions and sins, and so they were dead and alienated from God.

Ephesians 2:12

without the Messiah. In contrast to the great blessings that come as a result of being "in Christ," at one time the Gentiles were outside Christ. That is, they had no hope of a coming Messiah who would make all things right.
excluded from the citizenship. Gentiles were not part of God's kingdom. Israel was a nation founded by God, consisting of His people, and Gentiles were outside that reality.
foreigners to the covenants. Not only did Gentiles have no part in God's kingdom, they also stood outside all the amazing agreements (covenants) God made with His people.
with no hope. During this particular historical era, the Roman world experienced a profound loss of hope.
without God. Gentiles had no effective knowledge of the one true God.

Ephesians 2:13

But now . . . by the blood of the Messiah. Paul pinpointed how this great change occurred. It is because of Jesus' death on the cross that union with God is possible.

Ephesians 2:14

our peace. Jesus brings peace; that is, He creates harmony between human beings and God. He also creates harmony between human beings.
the dividing wall of hostility. Paul might have in mind an actual wall that existed in the temple in Jerusalem, beyond which Gentiles could not go. They were cut off by a stone wall, bearing signs in Greek and Latin that trespassing foreigners would be killed.
hostility. The ancient world abounded in hostility. There was enmity between Jew and Gentile, Greek and barbarian, men and women, slave and free. Christ ends each form of hostility.

Ephesians 2:16

reconcile. Literally, *to bring together estranged parties.* Here the reference is to bringing both Jews and Gentiles together with God.

Ephesians 2:17

He proclaimed the good news of peace. His first words to the stunned apostles after His resurrection were "Peace to you!" (John 20:19).

Ephesians 2:19

foreigners. Nonresident aliens were disliked by the native population and often held in suspicion.
strangers. These are residents in a foreign land. They pay taxes, but have no legal standing and few rights.
fellow citizens. Whereas once the Gentiles were "excluded from the citizenship of Israel" (v. 12), now they are members of God's kingdom.
members of God's household. In fact, their relationship is far more intimate. They have become family.

Ephesians 2:20

cornerstone. The stone that rested firmly on the foundation and tied two walls together, giving each its correct alignment.

Ephesians 2:21

fitted together. Used by a mason to describe how two stones were prepared so that they would bond tightly together.
sanctuary. The new temple is not like the old one, carved out of dead stone—beautiful, but forbidding and exclusive. Rather, it is alive all over the world, inclusive of all, and made up of the individuals in whom God dwells.

Notes

10

Notes

Session

11 PRAYING FOR ONE ANOTHER

Connections Prep

MAIN "LIFEPOINT": Prayer changes our community and us.

To reinforce the "LifePoint," leaders and small-group facilitators should understand the following more detailed CheckPoints and "Do" Points.

BIBLE STUDY CHECKPOINTS:

- Consider what James states about the effectiveness of praying for each other.
- Appreciate the role praying for each other plays in developing a redemptive community of faith.
- Focus on the areas of greatest need as we pray for those within our relationships.

LIFE CHANGE "DO" POINTS:

- Pray for each person in this group daily.
- Focus on one person in your church who has a serious illness and pray for them.
- Keep a journal of prayer victories and report them to this group.

PREPARATION:

- ☐ Review the leader book for this session and prepare your teaching in advance.
- ☐ Determine how you will divide students into small discussion groups.
- ☐ Recruit mature students or adults as small-group facilitators. Be sure these facilitators plan to attend your meeting.

REQUIRED SUPPLIES:

- ☐ *Contagious Community: Living Beyond Yourself* leader book for each group facilitator
- ☐ *Contagious Community: Living Beyond Yourself* student book for each student
- ☐ Pen or pencil for each student

"Get Ready" is primarily for students, but leaders and facilitators will benefit from these devotionals as well.

Get Ready

Read one of these short Bible passages each day, and spend a few minutes of focused time with God. Be sure to jot down any insights you receive.

MONDAY

Read James 5:13.
What are you more likely to do—pray when you face troubling situations or sing praises when you are happy? Why are they both important?

TUESDAY

Read James 5:14.
When was the last time you prayed for someone who was sick? Did you pray for them truly believing your prayer could make a difference? Why or why not?

WEDNESDAY

Read James 5:15.
From what in your life do you need spiritual healing? From what do you need physical healing? What is keeping you from bringing your needs before God right now? Talk to Him about your needs and concerns.

THURSDAY

Read James 5:16.
Who in your life is someone you consider "righteous"? Who is someone you can confide in? Whom do you trust enough to confess to? How important is it for you to find someone with whom you can share your downfalls?

FRIDAY

Read James 5:17-18.
Do you believe your prayers could change the course of natural events? Why or why not? What would you want God to change through your prayers? Would this benefit yourself or others?

SATURDAY

Read James 5:19-20.
Who is someone you know who needs to turn his or her life around? What can you do to help this person?

SUNDAY

Read Matthew 7:7-8.
Are you missing opportunities to do things for God because you aren't coming to Him in prayer? What would help your prayer life?

LARGE-GROUP OPENING:
Get everyone's attention. Make announcements. Open your session with a prayer. Read the "LifePoint" to students.

LifePoint

Prayer changes our community and us.

SMALL-GROUP TIME:
Instruct students to divide into groups of four to eight, preferably in a circle configuration.

Call on the mature student or adult leaders you recruited to facilitate each small group through this "Say What?" segment.

Say What? (15 minutes)

Random Question(s) of the Week:
What was the last song you purchased? What was the last song you listened to?

Group Experience: Superpowers
Share the following questions with the students in your small group and allow each student to answer. Encourage students to share their answers to the questions. The purpose of this experience is to allow students to share their thoughts with the group and also begin thinking about the groups with whom they spend their time.

1. Who was your favorite superhero as a child? Why did you like him or her?

2. What superpower would you most like to have right now? Why?
   - ☐ To read others' minds
   - ☐ To fly high above it all
   - ☐ To move from one place to another instantly
   - ☐ To have super-strength—to defeat the bad guys
   - ☐ To be invisible

- ☐ To control other people's minds
- ☐ To be able to turn back time
- ☐ Other ______________________________

3. What problem or need would you use your superpower to address?

LARGE-GROUP TIME: Direct students to turn to face the front for this teaching time. Be sure you can make eye contact with each student in the room. Encourage them to follow along and take notes in their student books.

So What? (30 minutes)

Share the "So What?" information with students. You may modify it to meet your needs. Be sure to highlight the underlined information, which gives answers to the student book questions and fill-in-the-blanks (shown in the margins).

Teaching Outline

I. Attitudes Toward Prayer

A. Look for God's hand at work in our lives

B. Choose to submit to God's will

II. Learning from the Bible

James 5:13-20

III. Prayer for Personal Concerns

IV. Prayer for Forgiveness

V. Prayer for Spiritual Direction

Attitudes Toward Prayer

❶ What are five attitudes people have toward prayer and its effectiveness?

Many times today when we speak of someone being in a desperate situation, we might say he or she "doesn't have a prayer." This means we feel that even prayer wouldn't be able to help this person out of his or her situation. Sadly, more often than not, we tend to believe that people are hopeless in their situations and prayer really won't change what they are going through. ❶ People today exhibit at least five attitudes toward prayer and its effectiveness. One is that prayer really never changes anything. It's something that we do when we can't do anything truly effective ourselves. At the time we pray, if we pray at all, it's because we can't do anything else and "it can't hurt." A second attitude is that prayer does have an effect, but only personally. It changes our attitude toward the problem and helps us draw on all our inner strength to address the problem. A third attitude is that prayer is simply to make us receptive and submissive to the will of God. It doesn't change what God is going to do, but rather it helps us to get in line with what God's will is for us. A fourth attitude is that prayer is like a magic wand that can bring whatever we ask, regardless of how it relates to God's Word, as long as we have enough faith. And a final attitude toward prayer is that it can change a situation, but only within the will of God. Whether or not we feel we truly "have a prayer" depends on which of these attitudes we have.

Looking at Scripture, we must understand that the last of the five attitudes listed above is the closest to the biblical perspective, while several others also have some merit. Prayer does change our attitude toward a problem. When Hagar was in the desert nearly dying with her son, she prayed and God opened her eyes to a nearby well, a resource she had previously not noticed (Genesis 21:8-21). Sometimes we become so wrapped up in a problem that we don't notice the resources available. And sometimes getting wrapped up in the problem can make us look past blessings we already have. We must see where God's hand is at work in our lives rather than focus on the areas where He is not.

❷ What is a biblical example of how prayer helps us to become more receptive to the will of God?

❷ Prayer also helps us to be more receptive to the will of God. Jesus' prayer in Gethsemane didn't change His immediate future. But after He prayed to be delivered from that "cup," He said, "nevertheless, not My will, but Yours, be done" (Luke 22:42). It was this prayer that helped Him say at the end, "Father, into Your hands I entrust My Spirit" (Luke 23:46). In the end, we have to remember that God is God and we are not. We must choose to submit to Him, not request Him to submit to us.

James encourages us to pray, believing in God's promises. However, he also calls us to do it within the context of submission to God. He calls us specifically in James 4:7 to, "submit to God." When we submit to God, we submit to His Will, and our prayers must reflect that. When we think it is more important for our own will to be done, that is when we try to use prayer as our own magic wand to control the world the way we think it should be.

❸ What are three kinds of needs people have for which James urges us to pray.

Because God wants the best for us, praying for what we need in context of God's will has great power. Like a great parent, God responds in love to all our requests. Even though He might not answer our prayers the way we want, he will respond with what we need—even if it hurts our feelings. ❸ James urges us to come to God in prayer for three kinds of needs: prayer for personal concerns, prayer for forgiveness, and prayer for spiritual direction. Let's look at each of these in our lesson.

Before the session, enlist a youth to read James 5:13-20.

Learning from the Bible

[13] Is anyone among you suffering? He should pray. Is anyone cheerful? He should sing praises. [14] Is anyone among you sick? He should call for the elders of the church, and they should pray over him after anointing him with olive oil in the name of the Lord.
[15] The prayer of faith will save the sick person, and the Lord will raise him up; and if he has committed sins, he will be forgiven. [16] Therefore, confess your sins to one another and pray for one another, so that you may be healed. The intense prayer of the righteous is very powerful. [17] Elijah was a man with a nature like ours; yet he prayed earnestly that it would not rain, and for three years and six months it did not rain on the land. [18] Then he prayed again, and the sky gave rain and the land produced its fruit.
[19] My brothers, if any among you strays form the truth, and someone turns him back,
[20] he should know that whoever turns a sinner from the error of his way will save his life from death and cover a multitude of sins.

Prayer for Personal Concerns

James encourages us to bring our personal concerns to God in prayer. He calls us in verses 13-15 to go to God in prayer when we are "suffering" or "sick." "Suffering" encompasses more than just physical suffering. The New International Version translates the word as "in trouble." So whatever kind of personal concern we are going through, we should go to God in prayer regarding it. In verse 15, he specifically states, in the case of sickness "The prayer of faith will save the sick person." Again, this must be done in the context of submission to God's will. ❹ Paul prayed for a problem he had and it was not cured. He described the problem as "a thorn in the flesh." In 2 Corinthians 12:8-9 he wrote, "Concerning this, I pleaded with the Lord three times to take it away from me. But He said to me, 'My grace is sufficient for you, for power is perfected in weakness.'" So it was made evident to Paul that it was not God's will he be healed of this, and Paul accepted and submitted to that will.

❹ What is a biblical example of someone who prayed for a physical need and was not healed, because it was not God's will at that time?

Many times when we see that prayers for those with physical ailments are not answered with healing, we become cynical. We conclude that prayer is useless and no one can be healed, so we give up and don't pray again. By similar logic one might say, "Never ask your friend to help you out, because sometimes they won't have time," or "Never ask your parents for help with your homework, because sometimes they will make you study harder." At least with God, when He doesn't give you what you ask for when you want it, we can point to divine wisdom concerning what is best for our lives.

The reality is that many people are healed because of prayer. Not only do we have the testimony of James that "The prayer of faith will save the sick person," ❺ but we have many biblical accounts of healing. Acts 5:16 states that, "a multitude came together from the towns surrounding Jerusalem, bringing sick people and those who

❺ What are two examples from Acts where people were healed?

were tormented by unclean spirits, and they were all healed." When Peter prayed for Dorcas, she was even raised from death (Acts 9:40-43). Within virtually every church, there are those who were told by doctors they had little hope for recovery yet found healing through the prayer of the faithful, but we discount the healing as a coincidence or proclaim how "lucky" the person is. We must see God's hand at work around us!

Perhaps the greatest tragedy of not praying for those who are sick is that we miss the opportunity to strengthen our fellowship with each other by praying. Praying for each other is a way of showing our love to one another. It shows that we care enough to link the person we are praying for to the very source of love and life itself!

Prayer for Forgiveness

James encourages us to pray for forgiveness of each other also. He tells us that when we pray for someone, "if he has committed sins, he will be forgiven" (v. 15). Many of us pray for our own forgiveness, but do we pray for the forgiveness of others? Do we pray for our family members' and friends' forgiveness? Praying for the forgiveness of each other is prayer that shows concern for each other's spiritual lives as well as each other's eternal condition.

❻ When we pray for the forgiveness of others, whose biblical example are we following?

❻ When we pray for each other's forgiveness, we also follow in the example of Christ. When His enemies were lifting Him up while He was on the cross, He prayed, "Father, forgive them, because they do not know what they are doing" (Luke 23:34). Many parents pray for the forgiveness and salvation of their children, siblings pray for each other, and children pray for their parents. When we are truly a family to each other, we also will pray for the forgiveness and salvation of those around us.

Prayer for Spiritual Direction

Finally, praying for the spiritual direction of the one who is wandering is a form of praying for each other that James encourages. In verses 19-20, he wrote "My brothers, if any among you strays from the truth, and someone turns him back, he should know that whoever turns a sinner from the error of his way will save his life from death and cover a multitude of sins."

The test of a contagious Christian community is not when everything is going well with everyone, but what it does when one or more of its members are struggling. One person stumbles in their sin. Another becomes ensnared in a relationship that has torn them away from their relationship with Christ. How does the community go about helping turn these friends back from their struggles? Are they condemned or expelled? That might push them further from Christ and His healing. Are they tolerated in a hushed sort of way where people try to ignore their problems but gossip about them behind their backs? That can encourage them to make believe nothing is wrong, or even worse, make them feel that they are alone with their problems, since no one even cares enough to acknowledge it. ❼ Certainly, prayer needs to be a central part of a contagious Christian community's support. However, it shouldn't just be prayer. Listening to the person, reaffirming biblical standards, and encouraging the person in his or her ability to meet those standards also needs to be part of the response. But prayer helps remind us and those struggling that God alone has the power to lift us above our human weaknesses. When Paul struggled with his own weaknesses, he cried out, "Who will rescue me from this body of death?" His response of faith was, "I thank God through Jesus Christ our Lord!" (Rom. 7:24-25).

❼ Besides prayer, what are three other ways we can help a person return from "the error of his way" (v. 20)?

On a number of occasions, Jesus said with God all things are possible (Matt. 19:23-26; Mark 9:21-27; 14:36). Prayer is the way God provides for us to reach beyond what is impossible and join in the possibilities of God—which are endless! Through prayer, people whom we have given up on are healed; through prayer, the laws of the natural world are bent to align with the will of God; through prayer, people who seem stuck in destructive life patterns miraculously find they can change their life's direction. It's all possible. But it is prayer that makes these things and more possible.

Certainly, we should not use such a powerful tool just on ourselves. When we use it for each other, we not only help people find freedom from illness and sin, but we help everyone to achieve a powerful, contagious Christian community that the world can find nowhere else.

SMALL-GROUP TIME: After presenting the teaching material, ask students to divide back into groups and discuss the "Do What?" questions. Small-group facilitators should lead the discussions and set the model for being open and honest in responding to questions.

Do What? (15 minutes)

Making It Personal

1. How should we pray for the sick, according to verse 15? How can we maintain this attitude in our prayer life?

2. What two things should a person do to be healed, according to verse 16? Which one do you most need to work on?

3. From what we have talked about today, what needs to be your next step in strengthening your prayer life?

Small-group facilitators should reinforce the "LifePoint" for this session, making sure that students' questions are invited and addressed honestly.

LifePoint Review

Prayer changes our community and us.

"Do" Points

These "Do" Points will help you begin to experience this week's "LifePoint." Be open and honest as you discuss the action points within your small group. Here are some actions to help you understand more about praying for others:

1. Pray for each person in this group daily. This is a part of the covenant we made at the beginning of our study, but this is a good time to renew our commitment to it. Since we have learned more about each other's lives in the course of this study, we should be able to pray more effectively for each other's lives, since we know each other better. Pray specifically for each person and the challenges they face in their life.

2. Focus on one person in your church who has a serious illness and pray for him or her. As teenagers, we have to look outside our circle of friends at times to find someone who is battling a long-term illness. Other times, we know someone in our school, church, or community who has a serious illness. Regardless of who it is, pray for that person every day this week. Let this person know that you are praying for him or her, and if possible, call to see how he or she is doing. Pay special attention to the prayer requests that are shared both in this group and outside.

3. Keep a journal of prayer victories and report them to this group. Part of seeing the benefits of prayer is knowing how prayer has changed things. We know how prayer is working when we share our victories with each other. If your group has been praying together for a specific need or challenge of yours, and you have benefited from that prayer or have had victory in your life, share that with your group. Regardless of the size of the victory you have, let others know how God is using their prayers in your life. This can bring your group closer together and encourage future prayers. Also, this allows you to see small victories in your own life, when many times we expect to see huge changes.

Encourage students to list prayer needs for others in their books so they can pray for one another during the week.

Assign a student coordinator in each small group to gather the group's requests and e-mail them to the group members.

Prayer Connection:

This is the time to encourage, support, and pray for each other in our journeys to trust God and seek out real and personal encounters with Him.

Share prayer needs and requests with the group, especially those related to hearing from and responding to God. Your group facilitator will close your time in prayer.

Prayer Needs:

Encourage students to dig a little deeper by completing a "Now What?" assignment before the next time you meet. Remind students about the "Get Ready" short daily Bible readings and related questions at the beginning of session 12.

Now What?

Remind them again this week that they are loved!

Deepen your understanding of who God is and His desire for us to have an authentic Christian community while we understand how our finances impact the world for Christ, and continue the journey you've begun today by choosing one of the following assignments to complete this week:

Option #1:

Keep a prayer journal this week. Keep both personal requests and the requests of others. Make notes of what you pray for and what others ask you to pray for. Also, keep a page reserved for answered prayers—and use it! When you see God's answer, whether it is what you expected or not, write it down. Be prepared to share your journal with the group next week.

Option #2:

Take time this week to re-write James 5:13-20 in your own words. Spend time reading the passage daily and write it in paragraph form. Be prepared to share your project with the group next week.

Bible Reference Notes

Use these notes to gain further understanding of the text as you study on your own:

James 5:14

sick. Especially in the first century, illness made one feel vulnerable. What could be done? Where could a believer go for help? James has an answer to this question.

call for the elders. Illness was to be dealt with in the context of the Christian community. The elders were to be called to minister to the ill person. They had two things to do: pray over the person and anoint him or her with oil.

anointing him with olive oil. When a Jew was ill, he or she first went to a rabbi to be anointed with oil. Oil was used not only for ritual purposes but also for cleaning wounds, for paralysis, and for toothaches.

James 5:15

the Lord will raise him up. James is quite clear about the source of the healing. It is not the oil; it is not the laying on of hands by the elders; nor is it even prayer in some magical sense. It is God who heals.

James 5:16

confess your sins. Confessing sins to one another removes barriers between people and promotes honesty in the Christian community.

James 5:17

man with a nature like ours. Elijah knew depression, despair, and doubt, just as did the Christians of James' time (1 Kings 19). Yet, God answered his prayer in a mighty way. Here James makes it clear that all Christians can pray like this, not just prophets.

James 5:18

the land produced its fruit. God controls the rain, and Christians can pray to Him to bring rain. By implication, while patiently enduring their troubles, Christians can pray in confidence to God about them.

notes

Session

12 Being Thankful for One Another

Connections Prep

MAIN "LIFEPOINT": We should be thankful for those God has put in our lives.

To reinforce the "LifePoint," leaders and small-group facilitators should understand the following more detailed CheckPoints and "Do" Points.

BIBLE STUDY CHECKPOINTS:

- Look at how Paul thanked God for the friends who worked with him.
- Consider the importance of thanking God for each other in developing a contagious Christian community.
- Look at some of the specific things for which we can be thankful in relation to each other.

LIFE CHANGE "DO" POINTS:

- Thank God daily for this group and what you have gained from being a part of it.
- Keep a journal of blessings.
- Tell one person not in this group why you thank God for him or her.

PREPARATION:

- ☐ Review the leader book for this session and prepare your teaching in advance.
- ☐ Determine how you will divide students into small discussion groups.
- ☐ Recruit mature students or adults as small-group facilitators. Be sure these facilitators plan to attend your meeting.

REQUIRED SUPPLIES:

- ☐ *Contagious Community: Living Beyond Yourself* leader book for each group facilitator
- ☐ *Contagious Community: Living Beyond Yourself* student book for each student
- ☐ Pen or pencil for each student

"Get Ready" is primarily for students, but leaders and facilitators will benefit from these devotionals as well.

Get Ready

Read one of these short Bible passages each day, and spend a few minutes of focused time with God. Be sure to jot down any insights you receive.

MONDAY

Read Philippians 1:3-4.
When you pray for others, who God has brought into your life for whom you are most thankful and joyful? Why? Have you told him or her?

TUESDAY

Read Philippians 1:5-6.
What is the work God has set before you? How could you be a part of making sure you "carry on to completion" the work God has set before you? With whom do you need to partner to make sure this happens?

WEDNESDAY

Read Philippians 1:7-8.
What can you do today to let the people who are important to you know how you feel about them? How have you been in the past with letting others know how you feel about them and what they have meant to you?

THURSDAY

Read Philippians 1:9-11.
How do you view others? Do you see them as rivals? Are you truly praying for them that they would be successful and that they would experience God's best for them? Why or why not?

FRIDAY

Read Philippians 1:12-14.

How has God used something that was tough for you personally to bring confidence to others? How do you feel when you are used to bring others confidence?

SATURDAY

Read Philippians 1:15-19.

Have you ever seen someone with false motives used by God? When? How do you feel when something like that happens to others?

SUNDAY

Read Philippians 1:20.

What can you do to honor Christ in the coming week?

LARGE-GROUP OPENING:
Get everyone's attention. Make announcements. Open your session with a prayer. Read the "LifePoint" to students.

LifePoint

We should be thankful for those God has put in our lives.

SMALL-GROUP TIME:
Instruct students to divide into groups of four to eight, preferably in a circle configuration.

Call on the mature student or adult leaders you recruited to facilitate each small group through this "Say What?" segment.

Say What? (15 minutes)

Random Question(s) of the Week:

Would you rather go a week without a shower or a week without changing clothes?

Group Experience: Chains

Share the following questions with the students in your small group and allow each student to answer. Encourage students to share their answers to the questions. The purpose of this experience is to allow students to share their thoughts with the group and also begin thinking about the groups with whom they spend their time.

1. What are things you would most like to be chained to, at least for a little while?
   - ☐ My cell phone—gotta stay connected!
   - ☐ My television—can't miss my shows!
   - ☐ My boyfriend/girlfriend—I need them!
   - ☐ The mall
   - ☐ The steering wheel of my car
   - ☐ My house—so I can finally rest!
   - ☐ Other ________________________________

2. What things in life have you felt most chained to?

3. How do you break away from something when you feel chained? Who has helped you most break free from the chains?

LARGE-GROUP TIME:
Direct students to turn to face the front for this teaching time. Be sure you can make eye contact with each student in the room. Encourage them to follow along and take notes in their student books.

Share the "So What?" information with students. You may modify it to meet your needs. Be sure to highlight the underlined information, which gives answers to the student book questions and fill-in-the-blanks (shown in the margins).

So What? (30 minutes)

Teaching Outline

I. Learning to Be Thankful
Supporting cast of team players

II. Learning from the Bible
Philippians 1:3-20

III. Friends Who Share in the Work
A. Directly
B. Through resources

IV. Friends Who Share in the Support
A. Emotional
B. Spiritual

V. Friends Who Pray

A. Support

B. Requests

Learning to Be Thankful

As you transition from the "Group Experience," say: **While we all have figurative chains, Paul was literally in chains during a good portion of his ministry. Nevertheless, he saw the positive side of what this experience did for the gospel. He was especially thankful for those Christian brothers and sisters who stood by him during this ordeal. We, like Paul, have people in our lives for whom we should be thankful.**

❶ What three things result from showing our thanks for one another?

❷ What can result from a leader's failure to acknowledge the need of others in order to be successful?

❸ With the exception of his letter to the Galatians, what does Paul always remember to do at the beginning of his letters?

❹ List at least five friends who were listed frequently by Paul in his writings.

Most of us know the importance of saying prayers of thanks to God for our blessings. Certainly, this is a central element in saying grace before meals: we want God to know how thankful we are for His faithfulness to give us food. ❶ Thanking each other does three important things: (1) it affirms our relationships as important. People who have helped us can know their contributions have been and continue to be valued; (2) it encourages positive behavior. Psychologists frequently point out that rewarding people for positive behavior is far more effective than criticizing or verbally attacking people for their negative behavior; (3) it serves as a reminder to us that we need other people. Sometimes people, especially those who are leaders, can get the idea that their accomplishments are solely the result of their own efforts. This is inaccurate, since we all depend on the contributions of others. Not even the greatest athlete in a team sport—whether it's Tom Brady, Dwayne Wade, Mia Hamm, or Alex Rodriguez—can win a championship on his or her own. ❷ even great leaders need a supporting cast of team players. If those who have successes do not acknowledge the help of others, then it sets them up to fail in the future.

Paul was a leader who knew the importance of saying thanks to those who helped him. ❸ In each of his letters, with the exception of Galatians, he begins by thanking those to whom he was writing. He knew, as we should, that in order to establish and maintain a contagious Christian community, we must express our gratitude to one another. Paul was constantly referring to his "friends" throughout his writings. ❹ Some of Paul's most notable friends are:

- Luke the physician—the one who traveled with Paul on many of his journeys and documented his accomplishments in the Book of Acts.
- Barnabas—the one who took great risks to reach out to a known persecutor of the church and trust him with leadership.

- Timothy—the young protégé who traveled with him and co-authored some of his letters.
- Lydia—the one who invited Paul and his followers into her home in Philippi.
- Priscilla and Aquila—who shared his profession of tentmaking, as well as his mission to carry the gospel to others.
- Silas—who traveled with him on his journeys after his dispute with Barnabas.

These are just some of the people whose names we know. If Paul would have designated a church where he had the most friends, he might have chosen the church at Philippi. Of the previously mentioned people, only Lydia was from there, but Paul spoke of this church with a special affection because of what he called their "partnership in the gospel." They had shared with him in several aspects of his work, and he was truly thankful.

❺ How did the Philippians help Paul?

❺ The Philippians were friends who had helped Paul in three different ways—by sharing in his work, by giving him emotional and spiritual support, and by praying for him. As we look at each of these, we will see both why he was thankful for them and what we need to show thankfulness for in our own friends.

Before the session, enlist a youth to read Philippians 1:3-20.

Learning from the Bible

3 I give thanks to my God for every remembrance of you, 4 always praying with joy for all of you in my every prayer, 5 because of your partnership in the gospel from the first day until now. 6 I am sure of this, that He who started a good work in you will carry it on to completion until the day of Christ Jesus. 7 It is right for me to think this way about all of you, because I have you in my heart, and you are all partners with me in grace, both in my imprisonment and in the defense and establishment of the gospel. 8 For God is my witness, how I deeply miss all of you with the affection of Christ Jesus. 9 And I pray this: that your love will keep on growing in knowledge and every kind of discernment, 10 so that you can determine what really matters and can be pure and blameless in the day of Christ, 11 filled with the fruit of righteousness that comes through Jesus Christ, to the glory and praise of God.

12 Now I want you to know, brothers, that what has happened to me has actually resulted in the advancement of the gospel, 13 so that it has become known throughout the whole imperial guard, and to everyone else, that my imprisonment is for Christ. 14 Most of the brothers in the Lord have gained confidence from my imprisonment and dare even more to speak the message fearlessly. 15 Some, to be sure, preach Christ out of envy and strife, but others out of good will. 16 These do so out of love, knowing that I am appointed for the defense of the gospel; 17 the others proclaim Christ out of rivalry, not sincerely, seeking to cause me trouble in my imprisonment. 18 What does it matter? Just that in every way, whether out of false motives or true, Christ is proclaimed. And in this I rejoice. Yes, and I will rejoice 19 because I know this will lead to my deliverance

through your prayers and help from the Spirit of Jesus Christ. [20] ***My eager expectation and hope is that I will not be ashamed about anything, but that now as always, with all boldness, Christ will be highly honored in my body, whether by life or by death.***

Friends Who Share in the Work

❻ What were two ways the Philippians shared in Paul's work?

First, Paul was thankful to the Philippians for sharing in his work. ❻ They shared in the work directly. Lydia, for instance, offered her home as a meeting place for the church in its infancy (Acts 16:11-5, 40). But they also shared in Paul's work by giving to it financially. Paul wrote, "And you, Philippians, know that in the early days of the gospel, when I left Macedonia, no church shared with me in the matter of giving and receiving except you alone. For even in Thessalonica you sent gifts for my need several times" (Phil. 4:15-16).

We need to show appreciation to friends who share in our work, whether it's hands on or through their resources. In the church, people have different things to offer. Some have the skills and energy to be up and moving around, while others have a limited amount of these resources. Some have very limited resources financially, while others have the ability to freely give to help support others in their endeavors. Many older people can no longer get around as they used to and they don't always have the energy to do the things they could once do. However, they may have some financial resources to contribute. On the other hand, many teenagers might be quite low when it comes to financial resources, but are more than willing to lend their hands and physical support to others. ❼ There are two very different attitudes we can have toward such contributions: we can look at what the person is not able to do and be critical, or we can look at what they are able to do and be thankful. Paul did the latter and that is a great example for us. As teenagers, we must be careful not to view others as simply financial contributors to what we are a part of, rather, we must view them in partnership with our physical actions and see the opportunity to thank them for helping us in God's work.

❼ What are two different attitudes we can sometimes have toward those who contribute out of their limited resources? What was Paul's attitude?

Friends Who Share in the Support

❽ What were three ways Paul needed support while he was in prison?

There is also the matter of emotional and spiritual support. ❽ Paul really needed that support in many ways during his imprisonment. He needed people to write to him. He needed people to come by and visit. He needed people to do things for him that he could not do for himself due to his physical restrictions. There were times when Paul did not have this support in an adequate way. In 2 Timothy 4:9-11, a letter also written while he was in prison, Paul pleaded, "Make every effort to come to me soon, for Demas has deserted me, because he loved this present world, and has gone to Thessalonica. Crescens has gone to Galatia, Titus to Dalmatia. Only Luke is with me." Paul's thankfulness for the Philippians was due in large part to the emotional and spiritual support they gave him. In 4:14 he wrote, "you did well by sharing with me in my hardship," and earlier in 4:10 he noted, "I rejoiced in the Lord greatly that now at last you have renewed your care for me." Certainly, the Philippians showed this concern in part by the financial gifts they gave, but to Paul it was equally important that they showed they were thinking about him in his time of need.

Very few Christians in our modern world have to go through imprisonment for their beliefs. Nevertheless, we live in a world that can be cold and unforgiving. Many songs today proclaim loneliness and the feelings of being deserted by others. We must realize that many people around us feel alone even when they are in the middle of a crowd. People don't necessarily find contentment in crowds of people. The struggles of a fallen world make life very difficult, but to feel isolated and alone makes this even more difficult. When we do have a caring friend who walks beside us, we must recognize their contribution to us and be thankful for their efforts to help. Again, we need to follow Paul's example to us in this area.

Friends Who Pray

A very specific kind of emotional and spiritual support comes when friends remember us in their prayers. Paul had a great confidence in the prayers of the Philippians, as he wrote in verse 19, "I know this will lead to my deliverance through your prayers and help from the Spirit of Jesus Christ." We talked in our last session of the importance of praying for each other, and here we need to remember the importance of thanking others when they pray for us. ❾ If we really believe in the power of prayer, we should believe this is one of the best things a person can do for us when we are going through stressful situations. When Jesus was in Gethsemane facing his imminent crucifixion and death, he didn't ask his closest friends to fight for Him—to the contrary He reprimanded Peter for doing so. Nor did He ask them to go out and buy things to console Him, or find Him a good lawyer. He simply asked them to wait with Him and pray (Matt. 26:36-41).

❾ When did Jesus model the importance of friends praying by His side in His time of need?

We can learn from Paul, but taking the time to thank people for their prayerful support. We must seek to have a caring Christian community that cares for us by praying for us. We must also be diligent in sharing our prayer requests with others and realize that prayers really do change our community and us.

SMALL-GROUP TIME: After presenting the teaching material, ask students to divide back into groups and discuss the "Do What?" questions. Small-group facilitators should lead the discussions and set the model for being open and honest in responding to questions.

Do What? (15 minutes)

Making It Personal

1. Why do you think Paul was so confident that the work of the Philippians would be "carried on to completion"?

2. Why was it important to Paul that the Philippians know his imprisonment had resulted in the advancement of the gospel?

3. In what way would you say your own "chains"—your own hard times—have served to advance the gospel or the good of others?

Small-group facilitators should reinforce the "LifePoint" for this session, making sure that students' questions are invited and addressed honestly.

LifePoint Review

We should be thankful for those God has put in our lives.

"Do" Points

These "Do" Points will help you begin to experience this week's "LifePoint." Be open and honest as you discuss the action points within your small group. Here are some actions to help you understand more about biblical giving:

1. Thank God daily for this group and what you have gained from being a part of it. Each day you can focus on a different aspect from which you have benefited. Thank God for specific people and experiences.

2. Keep a journal of blessings. At the end of each day, write in your journal the blessings you experienced during the day. It's fine to pray about the things that didn't go well, but in the journal focus exclusively on how God blessed you that day. If you go through a difficult experience, it's good to write about how God is already using it as a blessing. Make sure you include the names of people who were part of this blessing. It's best to do this at the end of the day, because it helps to end the day on a positive and thankful note.

3. <u>Tell one person not in this group why you thank God for him or her.</u> Make sure your comments are sincere. Choose a person who isn't a member of this group so your words might be used to encourage him or her. If possible find someone who struggles with their self-esteem and concentrate on finding a way to build him or her up.

Encourage students to list prayer needs for others in their books so they can pray for one another during the week.

Assign a student coordinator in each small group to gather the group's requests and e-mail them to the group members.

Prayer Connection:

This is the time to encourage, support, and pray for each other in our journeys to trust God and seek out real and personal encounters with Him.

Share prayer needs and requests with the group, especially those related to hearing from and responding to God. Your group facilitator will close your time in prayer.

Prayer Needs:

Encourage students to dig a little deeper by completing a "Now What?" assignment before the next time you meet.

Remind students about the "Get Ready" short daily Bible readings and related questions at the beginning of session 13.

Now What?

Remind them again this week that they are loved!

Deepen your understanding of who God is and His desire for us to have an authentic Christian community while we understand how our finances impact the world for Christ, and continue the journey you've begun today by choosing one of the following assignments to complete this week:

Option #1:

If you enjoy writing, write a letter to someone you are thankful for. You can choose a parent, teacher, friend, or church leader. Take time to write why you are thankful for this person and what they have done to influence you in your life. Put the letter in an envelope and either mail it to them or give it to them personally.

Option #2:

Take some time this week and re-write Philippians 1:3-20 in your own words. Feel free to paraphrase the passage or rewrite it in a paragraph form. The important thing is to grasp and communicate the meaning of the passage. Be prepared to share your thoughts next week with your small group.

Bible Reference Notes

Use these notes to gain further understanding of the text as you study on your own:

Philippians 1:3

for every remembrance of you. This is a difficult phrase to translate from the Greek. What it seems to mean is that Paul gave thanks for his Philippian friends regularly.

Philippians 1:4

always praying. This is not the usual Greek word for prayer, which is used in verse 9. This word carries the idea of *need* or *lack,* and means *intercessory prayer.* Paul was not just praying in general for the Philippians. He was praying God would meet specific needs that he knew they had.
with joy. "Joy" is a theme that pervades Philippians. This is the first of some 14 times that Paul used the word in this epistle. He mentioned "joy" more often in this short epistle than in any of his other letters. It is interesting his first reference to joy is in connection with prayer.

Philippians 1:5

because of your partnership. Paul was grateful to God for the Philippians, because they had always stood by him in the work of the gospel. The Greek word rendered as "partnership" is the familiar word *koinonia,* translated elsewhere as "fellowship." It means, literally, *having something in common.* It was a favorite word of Paul's. Of the 19 times it appears in the New Testament, he used it 13 times.
in the gospel. The Philippians were partners with Paul in spreading the gospel. Specifically, they supported him financially in his ministry (2:25; 4:10-20). In addition, they worked with him to spread the gospel (4:3); they prayed for him (1:19); they contributed generously to the fund he raised in aid of the needy Christians in Jerusalem (2 Cor. 8:1-5). The word "gospel" is another favorite of Paul's. He uses it 60 of the 76 times it appears in the New Testament. The "gospel" is the good news about what God has done in Christ Jesus to save men and women.

Philippians 1:6

I am sure of this. Confidence is another underlying theme of Philippians. Paul makes it very clear what lies at the root of this confidence. It is not human accomplishment or ritual of any sort (3:3-4). This is confidence that springs out of faith in who God is and what He is doing.
the day of Christ Jesus. This is the moment when Christ will return in glory and triumph to establish His kingdom on earth.

Philippians 1:7

because I have you in my heart. The phrase could also be translated, "because you hold me in such affection" (NEB). In this case, the way Paul felt about the Philippians was based on their affection for him. Perhaps the phrase is intended to be ambiguous and read both ways, since there was a mutuality of affection between Paul and the Philippians.
in the defense and establishment of the gospel. These are legal terms. The reference is to Paul's defense before the Roman court, in which he hoped not only to vindicate himself and the gospel from false charges, but to proclaim the gospel in life-changing power to those in the courtroom. (See Acts 26 for an example of how Paul did this when he stood in court before Agrippa and Festus.)

Philippians 1:8

God is my witness. In moments of deep feeling, Paul would sometimes invoke God to bear witness to the authenticity of those feelings (Rom. 1:9; 2 Cor. 11:11,31; 1 Thess. 2:5).
I deeply miss. This is yet another word characteristic of Paul. He used it seven of the nine times it is found in the New Testament. This is a strong word and expresses the depth of Paul's feelings for them, his desire to be with them, and the wish to minister to them.

Philippians 1:9

And I pray this. Paul's love for the Philippians led him to pray on their behalf. What he prayed is that they would overflow with love. He prayed this love will increase (go on developing) and that it would be regulated by knowledge and discernment.

Philippians 1:10

so that you can determine what really matters. The Philippians were confronted with competing ideologies as to what is true and how to live. They needed "knowledge" and "insight" in order to choose and follow that which is of God and so results in "purity" and blamelessness." The word translated "determine" is used to describe the process of testing coins so as to distinguish between those that are real and those that are counterfeit.

Philippians 1:12

I want you to know. This is a standard formula used in personal letters to indicate the writer is now going to provide some information about his or her circumstances. Paul assured them that good was coming out of his imprisonment. He did not at this point say much about the actual conditions of his imprisonment or the progress that had been made in terms of his forthcoming trial (perhaps it was dangerous for him to put such information in a letter). However, he did assure them that all this had had a positive effect on the spread of the gospel.
brothers. This is a generic term and means *brothers and sisters.* By this term, Paul indicates the nature of his relationship with the Philippians. He and they were all part of one, big family—God's family. "Brothers" is another favorite term of Paul's. He used it 133 times in his letters.
advancement. A word used to describe an army that is marching forward despite obstacles. Paul's imprisonment could have had a negative effect on the spread of the gospel. After all, here he was—the key evangelist—incarcerated and thus unable to get on with the preaching of the gospel in the towns and the cities of the Roman world. Furthermore, his imprisonment could have cast a shadow over his message, with potential converts concluding there was something criminal about what he was teaching. But the imprisonment had the opposite effect. People saw that this message was worth suffering for.

Philippians 1:13

imperial guard. These men were the elite soldiers in the Roman army, the bodyguards of the emperor. Because Paul had been sent to Rome for a hearing before the emperor, they were given the task of guarding him. Paul's guards changed every four hours or so, and thus he got the chance to witness to a rotating coterie of soldiers from the key regiment in Rome. News of who he was and what he stood for apparently spread through the barracks and beyond into official circles. In 4:22, Paul mentioned that some of those from Caesar's household had actually become Christians.
imprisonment. Paul was not in a jail, but rather in a rented house where he was able to receive visitors, correspondence, and gifts (Acts 28:16,30; Phil. 4:18). However, he was bound to a guard by a short chain that ran from his wrist to the guard's wrist. In such circumstances, it is not surprising that the guards got to know him and his gospel.

Philippians 1:14

Because of Paul's example, other Christians had become bolder in their own sharing of the gospel, and so they were spreading the message to even more people.

Philippians 1:15

Some. Although "most" (v. 14) of the brothers and sisters have been inspired by Paul's example to be bolder in proclaiming the gospel, "some" had used this imprisonment as the opportunity to advance their own honor, prestige, or cause. However, Paul still considered these people to be "brothers." He may not like what they were doing, but he did not reject them as members of God's family.
envy and strife. These people were motivated by some kind of grudge or hostility directed against Paul. They did not like him and wanted to hurt him by their preaching. What lay behind this animosity is not clear. Perhaps they looked on Paul in disdain because he was in jail, seeing this as a judgment from God against him. Or maybe they were jealous of Paul's role as an apostle and saw this as a golden opportunity to advance their own positions and prestige.

Philippians 1:17

rivalry. The Greek word translated "rivalry" has an interesting history. It originally meant a *day laborer.* It came to mean *someone who did sordid work.* It was used in the political realm to describe a person who had a partisan spirit. Eventually, it came to refer to a relentless careerist who would do almost anything to promote his or her own advancement.

Philippians 1:18

Christ is proclaimed. The one fact that makes it possible for Paul to accept this situation – and in fact to find positive value in it – is that whatever else might be said about these wrongly motivated brothers and sisters, the message still centers on Christ.
And in this I rejoice. This is an unexpected conclusion to Paul's report on his imprisonment. One might have expected an appeal that they pray for him in his difficult circumstances or that they work to get him released. This exclamation of joy is not how most people would sum up the experience of being in prison. But Paul has learned to see his circumstances in the light of God's plan; so what matters is not how comfortable he is but whether the gospel is thriving – and since it is, Paul can rejoice!
Yes, and I will rejoice. Here he prepares to give his second reason for rejoicing: He expects to be delivered from prison.

Philippians 1:19

I know. How he "knows" all this will result in his deliverance is not certain. Probably what he is referring to is a deep inner conviction that God will make right this situation. His confidence is based on two factors: their prayers and the work of the Holy Spirit.

Philippians 1:20

eager expectation. This is a rare word, used only here and in Romans 8:19. Paul expected God would give him the grace so that he would not be put to shame in his confession here and now. Paul hoped that he would have the courage to live or die as a true Christian should.

ashamed. This is another rare word. In the New Testament, it is used only here and in 2 Cor. 10:8. But unlike "eager expectation," this word is used in other literature, including the Old Testament. Depending on where one puts the "that," this means he is worried he might disgrace either himself or the gospel when he gets into court by not giving a proper defense.

boldness. What Paul desires is the courage to speak boldly during his trial. This same word is used Ephesians 6:19-20, where Paul expresses the identical desire.

highly honored. This word means, literally, to make something or someone large. When Paul uses this verb, he does not mean his trial will succeed in making Christ greater, but rather it will serve to make Christ, who is great, known to a larger audience.

notes

Session

13 REJOICING WITH ONE ANOTHER

Connections Prep

MAIN "LIFEPOINT": We choose to rejoice by finding the positive God has allowed in each situation.

To reinforce the "LifePoint," leaders and small-group facilitators should understand the following more detailed CheckPoints and "Do" Points.

BIBLE STUDY CHECKPOINTS:

- Appreciate the importance of rejoicing with one another in a contagious Christian community.
- Look at the role worry plays in taking us away from a spirit of rejoicing.
- See why it is important to focus on the positive in order to rejoice more and worry less.

LIFE CHANGE "DO" POINTS:

- Participate in worship with a purposeful attitude of celebration.
- Sing a song of rejoicing and praise at least once this week away from a "worship" service at church.
- Point out reasons for rejoicing to a friend.

PREPARATION:

- ☐ Review the leader book for this session and prepare your teaching in advance.
- ☐ Determine how you will divide students into small discussion groups.
- ☐ Recruit mature students or adults as small-group facilitators. Be sure these facilitators plan to attend your meeting.

REQUIRED SUPPLIES:

- ☐ *Contagious Community: Living Beyond Yourself* leader book for each group facilitator
- ☐ *Contagious Community: Living Beyond Yourself* student book for each student
- ☐ Pen or pencil for each student

"Get Ready" is primarily for students, but leaders and facilitators will benefit from these devotionals as well.

Get Ready

Read one of these short Bible passages each day, and spend a few minutes of focused time with God. Be sure to jot down any insights you receive.

MONDAY

Read Philippians 4:4.
What do you spend more of your time doing, worrying or rejoicing? Why?

TUESDAY

Read Philippians 4:5.
How can you let your graciousness be known to others? Are you doing it?

WEDNESDAY

Read Philippians 4:6.
How much time and energy do you spend on worrying? What have been the benefits of worrying? How can you transform your worry to prayer?

THURSDAY

Read Philippians 4:6-7.
Is your prayer life changing your life? Do you have more or less peace because of your time spent praying? What could help you with your worries?

FRIDAY

Read Philippians 4:8.

Do you choose to focus your thoughts on the negative or the positive? What do you do when you recognize your thoughts have turned to the negative? What are the benefits of focusing on the negative?

SATURDAY

Read Philippians 4:9.

How have you sensed the God of peace working in your life this week? What can you do today to be a witness for Christ?

SUNDAY

Read Nehemiah 8:10.

How have you found strength from your faith in the recent weeks? How has this impacted your life?

LARGE-GROUP OPENING:

Get everyone's attention. Make announcements. Open your session with a prayer. Read the "LifePoint" to students.

LifePoint

We choose to rejoice by finding the positive God has allowed in each situation.

SMALL-GROUP TIME:

Instruct students to divide into groups of four to eight, preferably in a circle configuration.

Say What? (15 minutes)

Random Question(s) of the Week:

When was the last time you laughed so hard you had to cover your mouth to keep stuff from flying out? What made you laugh so hard?

13

Call on the mature student or adult leaders you recruited to facilitate each small group through this "Say What?" segment.

Group Experience: Celebrate

Share the following questions with the students in your small group and allow each student to answer. Encourage students to share their answers to the questions. The purpose of this experience is to allow students to share their thoughts with the group and also begin thinking about the groups with whom they spend their time.

1. What causes you to celebrate?
   - ❑ When my team wins!
   - ❑ When the latest video game system comes out!
   - ❑ When I get good grades.
   - ❑ Knowing that a special friend is coming to visit.
   - ❑ Getting to go to the mall with my family.
   - ❑ Getting a pimple the day before school pictures—and then it vanishes overnight.
   - ❑ Other ____

2. When is the last time you celebrated? What caused you to celebrate? How did you celebrate?

3. How often do you worry? What do you worry about? What does worrying do for you?

LARGE-GROUP TIME: Direct students to turn to face the front for this teaching time. Be sure you can make eye contact with each student in the room. Encourage them to follow along and take notes in their student books.

So What? (30 minutes)

Teaching Outline

I. What Is "Rejoicing"?

A. Reasons to celebrate

B. Something to be cultivated

II. Learning from the Bible

Philippians 4:4-9

III. Winning Over Worry

Prayer

Share the "So What?" information with students. You may modify it to meet your needs. Be sure to highlight the underlined information, which gives answers to the student book questions and fill-in-the-blanks (shown in the margins).

IV. Focusing on the Positive
A. What God has already done
B. His promise to do more in the future

V. Practicing Our Faith
A. Live it out
B. Eliminate worry

What Is "Rejoicing"?

❶ Why should Christians have parties and celebrations?

When you think of a party, do you often think about it in relation to God? Most of us wouldn't think God and parties mix. We must admit the word "party" can take on many different meanings—running from the innocent gathering of a few people to the outlandish immoral events some teenagers are known for. Perhaps we must realize however, ❶ life does need to have its parties. God has given us a good gift in this life and it needs to be celebrated! Paul calls us to "Rejoice in the Lord always." Are we just to do that in a somber way, whispering "whoopee" under our breath? We must recognize that we have such a great gift that it deserves to be celebrated—and we have the duty to celebrate that responsibly. This can be a great indication of the joy that lives within Christians and can be a huge attraction to those who don't yet know Christ.

❷ What are two opportunities where Christians can celebrate their faith?

The truth is that a somber crowd seldom attracts anyone. That's possibly why more people attend the Super Bowl than attend the world championships of chess. If a group has to keep their emotions constantly under wraps and has very little to be excited about, why would others want to join them? This is not to say we should forget our responsibilities or the more serious issues of the world. Christians are called to be caring servants in the world; however, Paul reminds us that it's alright, and even important, to ❷ celebrate our faith. We can do that in worship experiences. We can also do that when we get together with Christian friends and enjoy fellowship together. We are a part of a joy-filled family—the family of God. So we must rejoice. Many people outside the church have in their minds that Christianity is oppressive and miserable, and many times they get their interpretation from Christians' faces! We have the keys to eternal life in a relationship with Christ—what could be a better reason to celebrate?

In Galatians 5:22, Paul listed "joy" as a part of the fruit of the Spirit. It certainly seems to be one of the more neglected "crops" of the Christian life. Even with biblical writers, Paul had his "love chapter" (1 Cor. 13), Hebrews had its "faith" chapter (Heb. 11), and much of the Books such as 1 Peter and Revelation are devoted to "hope." Where is a chapter on "joy"? The Book of Philippians addresses the issue of joy very well. At the beginning of the letter, Paul wrote of "praying with joy" (1:4). Then in 1:25, he wrote of how he hoped his continued presence in this life would bring the Philippians "joy in the faith"; in 2:2, he asked the Philippians to "fulfill my joy by thinking the same way"; in 2:29, he asked them to welcome Epaphroditus "with all joy." In 2:17-18, he spoke of how he rejoiced with the Philippians and wants them to rejoice with him. And in 3:1, Paul gave his first call for the Philippians to "rejoice in the Lord," a call that is echoed in our focal passage in 4:4. ❸ Joy has to be cultivated. Paul was seeking to cultivate it in the Philippians. Likewise, we need to cultivate it in our churches, classes, and Christian communities. Doing so requires that we work on the three skills that Paul alluded to in Philippians 4: (1) winning over worry; (2) focusing on the positive rather than the negative; and (3) practicing our faith. Paul knew that joy was possible. ❹ The truly fascinating thing about Paul's words to the Philippians about joy and rejoicing is that Paul wrote these words from jail, at a time that might not have been long before he was executed for his faith.

❸ What are the three skills that can help us cultivate joy in our life?

❹ What was special about the place and time that Paul wrote the letter of Philippians in relation to his message about joy?

Before the session, enlist a youth to read Philippians 4:4-9

Learning from the Bible

4 Rejoice in the Lord always. I will say it again: Rejoice! 5 Let your graciousness be known to everyone. The Lord is near. 6 Don't worry about anything, but in everything, through prayer and petition with thanksgiving, let your requests be made known to God. 7 And the peace of God, which surpasses every thought, will guard your hearts and your minds in Christ Jesus.

8 Finally brothers, whatever is true, whatever is honorable, whatever is just, whatever is pure, whatever is lovely, whatever is commendable—if there is any moral excellence and if there is any praise—dwell on these things. 9 Do what you have learned and received and heard and seen in me, and the God of peace will be with you.

Winning Over Worry

Because nothing robs us of our joy like worry, finding joy requires us to deal with this opponent. Paul wrote, "don't worry about anything" (v. 6). By making that statement, he conjured the words of Christ, "Don't worry about your life, what you will eat or what you will drink; or about your body, what you will wear" (Matt. 6:25). A common response to this teaching is that it is easier said than done! ❺ The key to winning over worry, is to learn to let go. Paul pointed to an important practice right away—prayer! He wrote in verses 6-7, "but in everything, through prayer and petition with thanksgiving, let your requests be made known to God. And the peace of God, which surpasses every thought, will guard your hearts and your minds in Christ Jesus." Turning our concerns over to God in prayer helps us to release them. It's kind of a spiritual cleansing. It's also reassuring to know that our Creator is working on our concerns and will do what is best for us.

❺ What essential practice does Paul point to in our test to help us deal with worry?

Focusing on the Positive

Paul encouraged the Philippians to win the battle over the mind by focusing solely on those things that bring God honor and meet His high standards rather than dwelling on those things that are negative or unholy. In verse 8 he wrote, "Finally brothers, whatever is true, whatever is honorable, whatever is just, whatever is pure, whatever is lovely, whatever is commendable—if there is any moral excellence and there is any praise—dwell on these things." This is Paul's equivalent of Jesus' "seek first the kingdom of God." The idea is that if we focus on the wonders of what God has already done, and the hope of His promise to do even more, then we won't concentrate and obsess so much over the bumps along the road. A story is told about Catherine the Great and her plans for the modernization of Russia. As part of her plan, Catherine the Great envisioned the construction of several great cities to serve as centers of industry and progress. During a state visit by the Austrian emperor Joseph II, the two rulers laid the foundation stones for one of these cities; Catherine laid the first stone and Joseph the second. Despite Catherine's enthusiasm, however, Joseph remained skeptical: "I have finished in a single day a most important business with the empress of Russia," Joseph later remarked. "She has laid the first stone of a city and I have laid the last." Sadly enough, the cities were never built. Much of our own worry amounts to this same thinking. If we look for the worst in a situation or expect ruin, we miss the recognition of how beautiful the day is and how great it is to be a child of God.

❻ Why is it important to have a supportive community in order to focus on the positive in life?

❻ The role of the community is absolutely vital in a venture directed at focusing on the positive. When all the people around us are griping and complaining, it's hard not to do the same. But we are drawn to a community where people are positive and celebrate the true, the honorable, the just, the pure, the lovely, and the commendable. Look back at the passage from session 1 in which it was said of that dynamic community of faith described in Acts, "They ate their food with gladness and simplicity of heart, praising God and having favor with all the people" (2:46-47). That is a positive community, and the kind we need to be like.

Practicing Our Faith

❼ Besides hearing a teaching, what are two things that need to happen before we really learn it?

We fight worry and learn to rejoice as we actually live our faith. Paul stated in verse 9, "do what you have learned and received and heard and seen in me, and the God of peace will be with you." ❼ Paul's statement accurately reflects how we learn. It's not just a matter of sitting and hearing a teaching. It's also a matter of (1) seeing that teaching lived out, not only in our teacher, but in the lives of other Christians around us. There is a story of a little boy who went to his father and asked, "Dad, when you were my age, did you go to church?" His father, quite proudly, responded, "Why yes son, I went every week without fail!" The son just shook his head and said, "Yeah, well, I bet it won't do me any good either!" We have to see

13

something practiced to believe it will do us some good! (2) Then we must receive it into our heart. We have to drop all of our emotional and intellectual barriers and let it affect how we think and live.

As we live our faith it becomes more real to us and to others. A few years ago a popular saying was, "Your 'talk' talks and your 'walk' talks. But your 'walk' talks louder than your 'talk' talks." This is true so much today in that people not only want to hear what we say makes us happy, they want to witness us actually being happy because of what we believe.

As we choose to live out our faith it becomes more real to us. It starts to affect how we think, how we act, and how we feel. When we choose to give our time, effort, energy, and money to a mission project, it helps us to reorient our thinking about what is important and release our anxieties about our abilities and our money. When we follow God's leading, even to sit with the kid who is alone at the lunch table, we learn to put our worries away a little more. We might not see our worries eliminated immediately, but we are beginning the process of releasing them to God.

Paul wrote to "Rejoice in the Lord always." He wasn't saying there won't be sad things that happen. He wasn't saying we must greet tragedy with a smile. But he was holding out for us an exciting possibility—the true joy of life doesn't come because of good circumstances or because there is nothing bad on the immediate horizon. It comes because we choose it as an act of faith—even when we don't immediately see the positive outcomes. We believe God always has something better in store, and that is always a good reason to choose to rejoice.

SMALL-GROUP TIME:
After presenting the teaching material, ask students to divide back into groups and discuss the "Do What?" questions. Small-group facilitators should lead the discussions and set the model for being open and honest in responding to questions.

Do What? (15 minutes)

Making It Personal

1. What is the connection between giving ourselves to the Lord (v. 5) and giving our resources to help with the needs of others?

2. How was Paul using the terms "rich" and "poor" in verse 9? How do we become "rich" through Christ's "poverty"?

3. What do you need to do at this point in your life in order to be more like the generous Macedonians and less like the more hesitant Corinthians?

Small-group facilitators should reinforce the "LifePoint" for this session, making sure that students' questions are invited and addressed honestly.

LifePoint Review

We choose to rejoice by finding the positive God has allowed in each situation.

"Do" Points

These "Do" Points will help you begin to experience this week's "LifePoint." Be open and honest as you discuss the action points within your small group. Here are some actions to help you understand more about rejoicing with others:

1. Participate in worship with a purposeful attitude of celebration. When you come into a planned worship service you come in with a choice. You can choose to celebrate what God is doing and has done in your life and in other's lives, or you can choose to watch the "performance." You have to choose to celebrate. The more you choose celebration, the more you will recognize opportunities for it.

2. Sing a song of rejoicing and praise at least once this week away from a "worship" service at church. Find a time and place to have your own celebration service for what God has done for you. It might be in the car on the way home from school (It's OK if others are there!) or it might be alone in your room after you spend time praying for this group. Regardless of when and where, find a time this week to celebrate God and His work away from a regularly scheduled "worship" service.

3. Look for an opportunity to point out reasons for rejoicing to a friend. When you choose to rejoice, often friends and even family members don't understand why. Look for an opportunity this week to share your "rejoicing" attitude with a friend. Explain to them what you have learned and why you are choosing to rejoice. You will be surprised at their reactions.

Encourage students to list prayer needs for others in their books so they can pray for one another during the week.

Assign a student coordinator in each small group to gather the group's requests and e-mail them to the group members.

Prayer Connection:

This is the time to encourage, support, and pray for each other in our journeys to trust God and seek out real and personal encounters with Him.

Share prayer needs and requests with the group, especially those related to hearing from and responding to God. Your group facilitator will close your time in prayer.

Prayer Needs:

Encourage students to dig a little deeper by completing a "Now What?" assignment.

Now What?

Remind them again this week that they are loved!

Deepen your understanding of who God is and His desire for us to have an authentic Christian community while we understand how our finances impact the world for Christ, and continue the journey you've begun today by choosing one of the following assignments to complete this week:

Option #1:

This week keep a journal of opportunities you have to rejoice. Keep a note of whether you chose to rejoice in the situation or not. Journal why you made the choice to either rejoice or not rejoice. Be prepared to share a few of these opportunities and your choices with the group.

Option #2:

Take some time this week and re-write Philippians 4:4-10 in your own words. Feel free to paraphrase the passage or rewrite it in a paragraph form. The important thing is to grasp and communicate the meaning of the passage. Be prepared to share your thoughts next week with your small group.

Bible Reference Notes

Use these notes to gain further understanding of the text as you study on your own:

Philippians 4:4

Rejoice. Paul returned to this central admonition that pervades the whole epistle. This is the first of a series of attitudes that make it possible to cope successfully in a hard situation. If one is rejoicing, one cannot be despairing. Paul is not calling for people to rejoice because of the situation. Rather, the Lord is the source and cause of rejoicing.

Philippians 4:5

The Lord is near. It is possible to rejoice and to act with graciousness because the Lord will return in the very near future and bring to an end all of one's trials and difficulties. The Lord is "near" in a second sense as well. He is close to His children, via the Spirit, aiding them as they face these difficulties.

Philippians 4:6

Don't worry. This is not a command given lightly. The Philippians certainly had cause to worry, and Paul, who wrote this command, was in prison. Yet to worry is to display a lack of confidence in God's care and in God's control over the situation (Matt. 6:25-34).
Prayer / petition / requests. Paul used three synonyms in a row to describe the alternative to anxiety. Instead of worrying, a person ought to converse directly with God and lay out before Him all that is on his or her mind, confident that God will hear and respond.

Philippians 4:7

the peace of God. This is the only time this phrase is used in the New Testament. It is part of God's inner character and what He experiences. Amazingly, it is this peace He offers to share with His children.
surpasses every thought. Human beings can never fully understand such peace. It is the peace that relieves anxiety in a way quite beyond what people can do on their own.
guard. This is a military term. It describes a garrison of soldiers, such as those stationed at Philippi, whose job it was to stand watch over the city and protect it.

Philippians 4:8

whatever is. Paul listed a series of virtues—perhaps drawn from the teaching of the philosophers of his day (since these are unusual words not used in this sense elsewhere in Paul's writings).

Philippians 4:9

There is a style of life that goes beyond pagan goodness. Ultimately, their behavior ought to reflect the commandments of God, which will at times be different from what popular culture commends.

Acknowledgements

We sincerely appreciate the great team of people who worked to develop this study on *Contagious Community: Living Beyond Yourself, Youth Edition.* Special thanks are extended to Keith Madsen for the content he composed for the adult version and to Mike Wilson for adapting the adult study for youth. We also appreciate the editorial and production team that consisted of Syble Groover, Jennifer Showalter, Beca Monger, and Katrina Bates.